DAVID ROCCO'S
DOLCE FAMIGLIA

DAVID ROCCO'S
DOLCE
FAMIGLIA

PHOTOGRAPHY BY FRANCESCO LASTRUCCI

HarperCollinsPublishersLtd

Published by HarperCollins Publishers Ltd

First edition

HarperCollins books may be purchased for educational, business
or sales promotional use through our Special Markets Department.

HarperCollins Publishers Ltd
2 Bloor Street East, 20th Floor
Toronto, Ontario, Canada
M4W 1A8

www.harpercollins.ca

Library and Archives Canada Cataloguing in Publication
information is available upon request.

ISBN 978-1-44344-526-9

Printed and bound in China
RRDSC 9 8 7 6 5 4 3 2 1

To Josie and Mimmo, my mom and dad.
Thank you for all your love and unconditional
support. You showed me the power of food, and
how cooking and eating together bring people
and families closer. Love you both!

CONTENTS

INTRODUCTION

Italians are famous for family gatherings. Around the world, it seems we all head over to Mamma's or Nonna's for Sunday *pranzo*, which is generally a feast of family favorite comfort foods. It's not that Italian families are better at getting along with each other than anyone else, but that the ritual of breaking bread together runs deep in the Italian psyche. And it's kind of genius, I think, because few things are as pleasurable as sharing a meal.

Making a meal—no matter how humble—sitting together around the table, taking time to enjoy the way the food looks and smells, and appreciating that someone put their time into making it can make you feel happier and more connected to each other, and to life.

Now, what I consider family doesn't always match the traditional definition. Because of distance some of us are far from our blood relatives, so we create our families where we live. After all, a family isn't just DNA. It's also a feeling. Is a group of friends who get together every so often to have a meal any less a family?

In my travels I've met many people who over the years have forged relationships as deep as any family. I'm thinking about the co-op group of fishermen I met in Orbetello, Italy, who eat together every day. To me, that's family. When I'm on the road shooting a show, my crew and I are like family. We end our day by sitting at the table and breaking bread together, at times talking through our differences.

So, this is the spirit I'm trying to capture in this book. It's about recipes that come from tradition. Recipes that I hope will bring you and your family—however you define family—together again and again to connect over a meal.

Dolce Famiglia is divided into two parts. The first part is about my family and what we eat on a regular basis. I have three little kids who have been brought up to eat what the adults eat, so they've come to love a range of foods. And like so many other families, when we have time to prepare a special meal, it's all about our version of comfort food—those recipes are included here, too.

The second part of the book is dedicated to some of the great families that I've met through my travels in Italy. Some people I met only briefly. Others have become lifelong friends. All of them invited me into their homes and their kitchens and have taught and inspired me.

The kind of food that I grew up on and that I love to cook isn't very fancy. My inspiration is the Italian *cucina povera,* or peasant food, tradition. For centuries, people had very little and their diets were limited to what they could grow or trade for. So, they ate with the seasons, because they had no other choice. Nothing went to waste—not a bit of stale bread or a vegetable past its best day. In *cucina povera,* every bit of food was made into something delicious. Even today when food is readily available, those *cucina povera* recipes are still hugely influential in Italy. So with that philosophy in mind, the recipes in this book are not complex—most take very little preparation time—but they are delicious.

And finally, cooking, for me, is a source of creative expression. And I think the cliché is true: Cooking is a way of expressing love and affection. But if someone made me read a recipe and cook exactly what was written down in terms of quantities and sometimes even directions, I'd never go into a kitchen again. I'm a bit of a rebel. And I encourage you to be one, too.

The quantities and directions set down in these recipes are the basics and make a good starting point. But cook to your tastes. You want more Parmigiano-Reggiano? Add more. You want less? Add less. Or substitute pecorino. Ingredients vary from region to region, season to season. Things may cook more slowly in your kitchen than in mine. My best advice is to keep your eye on what you're cooking and to make it your own.

When you cook from this book we start the meal together, but you end it where you want to. Cooking is, after all, your expression. And your gift to your family and friends.

KITCHEN
NOTES

QUANTO BASTA

When an Italian is giving you directions for making something, they'll use the term *quanto basta*. It means "use as much as you want" or "as much as you need and no more."

There are a few things I like about that. It's a reminder that you are the master of your own dish and that you should always adapt it to your tastes. Ingredients change from batch to batch, region to region, season to season. If it's the height of summer and your ingredients are luscious and fresh, you might naturally alter proportions slightly just because things taste different.

When you see "QB" in this book, it means that you choose how much of that ingredient you want for the recipe.

Quanto basta is also a great metaphor for living a balanced life: Use what you need, no more, and leave something for another person and another day. It's a wise philosophy from the mouths of *nonne*.

EXTRA-VIRGIN OLIVE OIL

For the most part, I use extra-virgin olive oil for everything, including frying. I know that it has a lower smoking point than some other cooking oils, but this is not a problem in my recipes. When you're frying, stay close to the stove and keep an eye on your pan, then add your ingredients when the oil starts to shimmer, so it never reaches its smoking point. So, in my kitchen you'll find a bottle of everyday or all-purpose extra-virgin olive oil for frying and cooking as well as a bottle of really, really good-quality extra-virgin olive oil. In Italy, everyone uses their best for things like salad dressing and for drizzling on finished dishes. Look for a bottle that shows you when the olives were harvested and gives you an expiry date; that way you'll know it's fresh and the taste will be vibrant. The good stuff will cost you more, but the taste and the way even a bit enhances the flavor of what you're eating are well worth it.

OLIO
EXTRA
VERGINE
D'OLIVA

EQUIPMENT

I have very little special equipment in my kitchen. The more stuff you use, the more you have to clean up, and who has time for that? Besides, I like to get my hands in and play with my food, so I tend to take a simple approach as often as possible. But there are times when it's nice to use a tool to make things a bit easier.

In my kitchen, the tools I use the most are a couple of heavy cutting boards and a great set of sharp knives. I recommend investing in the best-quality knives you can afford.

If you want to make fresh pasta, which I recommend, then you might want to get yourself a hand-crank pasta maker. After a few tries, you'll be a master pasta maker and wonder why you ever doubted yourself.

If you want to make filled pasta like ravioli, you need to use a pasta, or pastry, cutter. This inexpensive little tool will seal your pasta and give it a nice crimped edge.

PASSATA

A lot of recipes in this book call for *passata*. Passata is simply plum tomatoes that have been picked at the peak of the season and then peeled, seeded and puréed. At one time passata was considered an "exotic" ingredient; now it's in every store. Look for brands that contain no salt or sugar, or other additives.

LEGUMES

In a pinch, using canned beans and other legumes is fine. They're actually a staple in my house. Just be sure to rinse them well under cold running water before adding them to a recipe, to get rid of the excess salt and preservatives. Dried legumes, however, will give you more flavor and they are easy to prepare. They just require some planning because they need to be soaked overnight before cooking. Here's the general technique:

The night before you're going to make them, rinse the beans well under running water, then place them in a bowl or a pot, cover with cold water and let them sit overnight on the counter. The next day, drain and give them another good rinse.

To cook the beans, place them in a pot and add enough cold water to cover the beans by about an inch (2.5 cm). Throw in a bay leaf, a couple of fresh sage leaves and a sprig of fresh rosemary. Put the pot on the stove, bring it to a boil and then reduce the heat and let the beans simmer until tender, about 45 minutes. Drain the cooked beans and discard the herbs. Now you're ready to add them to your recipe.

If you plan to store the cooked beans in the fridge, don't drain the water. The beans will keep in their cooking liquid for a few days. Cooked beans also freeze nicely (drain well before freezing).

PASTA

COOKING PASTA AND SAUCES

Many of the pasta sauces in this book can be made in about the same time that it takes to cook the pasta. So put the pot of water on to boil when you start making your sauce. By the time the water boils and you put the pasta in, your sauce will be well under way and ready to receive the pasta when it's al dente.

But remember—this is important—you never want your pasta to be ready before your sauce or the pasta will end up overcooked. So if your sauce has to sit for a minute or two, or even more, that's perfectly fine and often even better. A few more tips:

- Always liberally salt the water when it's boiling, just before you add the pasta.
- Never add oil to the cooking water unless the recipe specifically says to.
- Cook your pasta until it's al dente. You want to cook it just until it is tender but still has a little bite, not boil it to the point where it's falling apart. My advice is to start testing your pasta 90 seconds before the package instructions say it's done. Take a bite, and if it's still too hard, keep cooking but test every 30 seconds or so until you find the right tenderness.
- You can buy pots with built-in strainers that allow you to remove the pasta from the cooking water without having to drain the water from the pot, and slotted spoons that let you lift the pasta out of the water. The advantage of these tools is that they keep the pasta water on hand in case you want or need to use it in the sauce. Often adding some of the cooking water to the sauce along with the pasta finishes the dish. The cooking water contains starches from the pasta that will help bind the sauce to the pasta. If you use a strainer to drain the water from the pot, just remember to reserve 1 cup (250 mL) of the cooking water before you let all that starchy loveliness disappear down the drain.
- Unless the recipe indicates otherwise, add the cooked pasta to the pan with the sauce and toss everything together. Let it cook for a minute so the sauce and pasta get to know each other a bit. That way the sauce will thicken up and cling to the pasta.

THE BASICS: PASTA

FREEZING PASTA

A number of recipes in this book call for fresh pasta. If you haven't ever made fresh pasta, I urge you to try. It's quite simple and the results are worth the effort.

Fresh pasta freezes beautifully. Simply arrange the pasta in a single layer on a baking sheet, making sure that none are touching, and then transfer the pan to the freezer. Once the pasta is frozen, transfer it to a freezer bag or airtight container. It will keep for up to 4 months. Frozen pasta can go directly from the freezer into boiling salted water.

FRESH PASTA DOUGH

4 1/2 cups (1.12 mL) all-purpose flour, plus more for dusting

6 eggs

1 tsp (5 mL) extra-virgin olive oil (optional)

Making fresh pasta is so much easier than you might imagine. For basic pasta, you need only two ingredients: eggs and flour. But I also recommend adding a little olive oil. It adds a bit of flavor. As for the quantities of these ingredients, I go by a 1:1 rule: 1 egg for every 3/4 cups (175 mL) of flour. In my family, we make about 3 1/2 oz (100 g) of pasta per person. I go full-on *nonna* for this recipe: I make it right on the counter, no bowls necessary.

Pour the flour onto the counter. Use your hands to make a little well in the middle, and then crack the eggs into the well. Add the oil if you're using it. With a fork, start beating the eggs. Once they're beaten, use your fork to start pulling the flour into the center from the sides, a little bit at a time.

Once the eggs and flour begin to come together, forming the beginnings of your dough, put the fork aside and use your hands to finish mixing everything together. Gather the dough and start kneading, using the palms of your hands to push the dough away and then roll it back toward you. Keep going with that push-and-pull motion. This is how you build elasticity in the dough. In about 5 minutes you'll end up with a nice cohesive, shiny ball of dough. You'll know it's ready when you can push your finger into the dough and the dough springs back.

Now you need to let it rest: Wrap the dough in some plastic and refrigerate it for half an hour.

After that you're good to go. Dust your work surface with a little flour and make your favorite pasta shape.

Cut off a piece of the raw dough (about the size of a tennis ball), use the palms of your hands or a rolling pin to flatten it out, and roll it through a pasta machine several times to produce a nice thin sheet. (See Using a Pasta Machine, page 16.) Don't let your dough dry out! Cover the parts that you're not using at the moment with a damp towel.

SERVES 6

USING A PASTA MACHINE

To put pasta through a pasta machine, flatten the dough with the palms of your hands or a rolling pin until it's about 1 inch (2.5 cm) thick. Sprinkle a little bit of flour on each side. With the rollers on the widest setting, run the dough through the machine. Fold the dough into thirds, like a pamphlet, press it lightly to flatten and roll it through the machine again, open side first. Do this a total of three times. If the dough sticks, dust it very lightly with flour—just enough to keep it from sticking.

Keep working this way, now running the dough through the pasta machine on increasingly thinner settings. Use your hand to guide the pasta out of the end of the machine so that it doesn't stick to itself. You'll know it's thin enough when you can see the outline of your hand through the dough.

When you achieve the thickness you want, you have two choices. If you're going to continue to use the machine, choose the attachment that will give you the shape you're after. A pasta machine will make any kind of long pasta. Or you can go full *nonna* and cut the pasta into long strips with a knife. Then you're ready to go.

If you're cooking the pasta immediately, lay it out on a damp towel so none of the strands are touching each other, and cover with another damp towel. Note that if you want to save the pasta for later, you have to let it dry for half an hour, making sure the strands don't touch. Then you can store it in airtight containers or resealable bags. Fresh pasta will last a few days in the fridge and longer in the freezer (see page 11). You can cook it straight out of the freezer.

THE BASICS: SAUCES

MY FAVORITES

There are tons of different pasta sauces, but as far as I'm concerned, the next four should be in everyone's repertoire: basic tomato sauce, ragù, Bolognese and pesto. They're super easy. They just take different amounts of time to make.

    With my family's roots in the south of Italy, tomato sauce and its derivatives play a big role in our favorite family meals. And as for pesto, I jokingly call it my Italian MSG because it's not just a great sauce for pasta, but a tablespoon (15 mL) added to certain dishes—soups or stews, for instance—can really bring them to life.

TOMATO SAUCE

1/4 cup (60 mL) extra-virgin olive oil

2 cloves garlic, crushed, or 1 small onion, minced

Dried chili flakes, QB (optional)

1 can (28 oz/796 mL) passata or whole plum tomatoes, squished by hand

Salt, QB

4 to 5 fresh basil leaves, torn

I've put this recipe in every one of my cookbooks because it's indispensable. It's been called Simple Tomato Sauce, Five-Minute Tomato Sauce, My Mother's Five-Minute Tomato Sauce . . . you get the point. It's simple, but so delicious, and it really does only take about 5 minutes to put together. In the time it takes to boil water and get your pasta cooking, the sauce is done. This recipe makes enough for about 1 lb (500 g) of pasta.

In a large frying pan or pot, medium heat, heat the olive oil. When it starts to shimmer, add the crushed garlic. (If you want, you can substitute 1 small onion for the garlic. If you like a bit of heat in your sauce, add some dried chili flakes.) When the garlic is just—*just*—starting to brown, pour in the passata or squished tomatoes. Increase the heat to medium-high and bring your sauce to a light bubble. Add some salt, reduce the heat to medium, and let it simmer for 5 minutes. Throw in some basil and you're done.

MAKES ABOUT 4 CUPS (1 L)

RAGÙ NAPOLETANO

1/4 cup (60 mL) extra-virgin olive oil, or more, as needed

Medium onions, diced, QB

Mixed cuts of stewing beef, QB

Beef and pork ribs, QB

Cotica, pork rinds or pork skin, QB

Beef or pork sausages, cut into pieces if large, QB

Meatballs (see page 100), QB

Red wine, QB

Passata, QB

Salt, QB

Freshly ground black pepper, QB

Every Sunday—whether we were at my mom's, aunt's or grandmother's house for *pranzo*—this sauce was mandatory. Even catching a whiff of it now takes me back to my childhood. It's a classic Neapolitan dish. Every family and restaurant in Naples serves it, and each has their own way of making it.

It's both simple and complex. It's simple because you throw everything in the pot and let the stove do the work for you. But it has a complex flavor profile that comes from the different cuts of meat simmering together in a tomato sauce. That's what makes this ragù so special.

A true ragù Napoletano has to be left to simmer for 5 to 6 hours, slow-cooked until the tomato sauce turns a very deep red and the meat is falling apart. In the end you will have made two dishes in one pot: a rich tomato sauce for your pasta and beautifully tender meat for your *secondo*.

There's nothing fancy here. This is all QB, so I don't provide the quantities. Just make sure you have enough passata to cover everything in the pot. Use 1 cup (250 mL) wine and 1 medium onion per 4 cups (1 L) of passata.

Heat the olive oil in a large stock pot over medium-high to high heat. Add the onion and all of the meat except the sausages and meatballs. Sear the meat on all sides. Add the wine. Once the wine has reduced by half, add the sausages and meatballs. Pour in enough passata so that the meat is entirely covered by a couple of inches (5 cm). Season with salt and pepper. Once the sauce starts to bubble, reduce the heat to low. Cover the pot and let the sauce simmer for 5 hours, occasionally stirring gently and skimming off any fat from the surface, if necessary.

After 5 hours, turn off the heat and let the ragù rest, covered, for about an hour. Using a slotted spoon, remove the meat from the sauce.

SERVES AS MANY AS YOU LIKE

BOLOGNESE SAUCE

1/4 cup (60 mL) extra-virgin olive oil

1 onion, finely chopped

1 stalk celery, finely chopped

1 large carrot, finely chopped

2 tbsp (30 mL) unsalted butter

1/2 lb (250 g) ground beef

1/2 lb (250 g) ground pork

1 cup (250 mL) dry white wine

1 cup (250 mL) milk

3 cups (750 mL) passata

Salt, QB

Even though Bolognese doesn't contain any meatballs, my son, Little D (aka Dante), calls this "my meatball sauce." It's his favorite sauce and, maybe because of that, it has become mine, too. It's rich and hearty, and it goes with any type of pasta. It also happens to be the sauce I use to make lasagna. (For that, increase the amount of passata to 5 cups/1.25 L and add 1 cup/250 mL of water.)

Heat the olive oil in a large pan over medium heat. When it starts to shimmer, add the onion, celery and carrots. Let them cook until soft and somewhat translucent, so the flavors come together and become sweet and intense. Add the butter and the ground beef and pork. Increase the heat to high. Cook, stirring frequently so that nothing sticks to the bottom of the pan, until the moisture in the meat has been released and the meat is lightly browned. Add the wine, stir again to pick up any bits on the bottom of the pan, and cook until most of the liquid has evaporated. Add the milk and cook until it has reduced by three-quarters. Then stir in the passata and salt. Reduce the heat to low and let simmer, stirring occasionally, for a few hours to let the flavors come together and intensify.

This sauce keeps well in an airtight container in the fridge for about a week. Or you can freeze it for up to 4 months. Be sure to cool it completely before storing.

SERVES 6 TO 8

Pesto is a very simple sauce in which a few ingredients are chopped together to form a paste and then olive oil is added to blend everything and give it more flavor and texture.

The beauty of pesto is that there are so many possible variations: use different herbs or nuts. *Pesto amalfitano*, for example, uses fresh parsley and walnuts. I've also seen nut-free and dairy-free versions, and some that omit the garlic. What I'm giving you here is a very basic basil pesto recipe that you can adjust to suit your tastes. For instance, sometimes I toast the pine nuts before I add them. It brings out a slightly deeper, nuttier flavor that I like.

Pesto isn't just for pasta, by the way. I think of it as a natural MSG. It adds an extra layer of flavor or a fresh hit of basil to so many dishes. Try adding a spoonful or two to soups and stews, or rub a bit on chicken or fish before cooking them. A little goes a long way.

Pesto is something you can make with your kids, especially if you don't have the patience for peeling garlic. That's a job they love.

PESTO GENOVESE

4 cups (1 L) lightly packed
fresh basil leaves

1/2 cup (125 mL) pine nuts
(lightly toasted, if desired)

2 cloves garlic

1 1/2 tsp (7 mL) coarse
sea salt

1 cup (250 mL) freshly
grated Parmigiano-
Reggiano

1 cup (250 mL) extra-virgin
olive oil

You can make pesto in a food processor if you prefer a smooth consistency. That's fine. Just whiz the basil, pine nuts, garlic and salt into a paste, then pulse in the Parmigiano and slowly drizzle in the olive oil. But I like to make it with a mezzaluna. It's easy and you get a much more interesting texture. Plus it's just more fun.

If you're using a mezzaluna, put the basil, pine nuts, garlic and salt on a large chopping board and then rock and roll the mezzaluna back and forth, mulching everything until it comes together. At this point, transfer it into a jar. Add the Parmigiano, and then pour in the olive oil. Seal the jar and shake well to mix it all together. Taste and adjust the seasonings.

If you're going to store it in the fridge for a while, top it up with olive oil so that the pesto is completely covered and then seal the jar. Your pesto will keep for a couple of weeks in the fridge this way. You can also portion it into ice-cube trays and freeze, then pop the cubes into freezer bags. They'll keep for about six months.

MAKES 2 TO 3 CUPS (500 TO 750 ML)

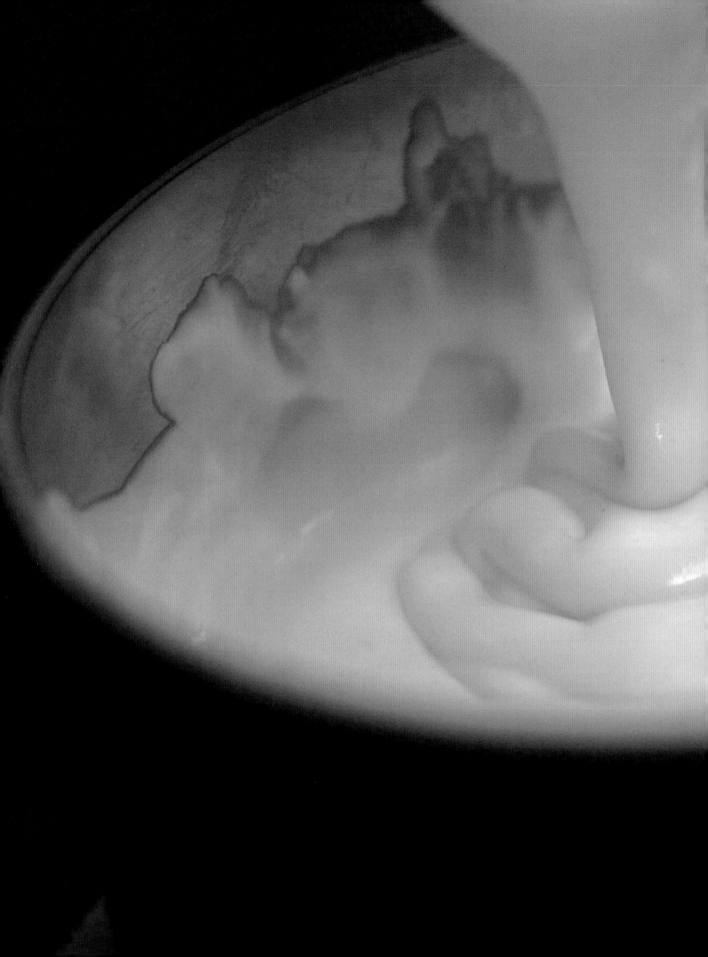

SALSA BESCIAMELLA

4 cups (1 L) milk

1/4 cup (60 mL) butter

1/4 cup (60 mL) all-purpose flour

Salt, QB

Freshly ground white pepper, QB

This is not one of my essential four sauces, but it's worth having in your hip pocket. Salsa Besciamella is a lush white sauce made with butter, flour and whole milk. It works with tortelli (page 330), tortellini (page 154), ravioli (page 131), and all kinds of other dishes the Emilia-Romagna region is famous for. It is also often used in lasagna.

You need two pots. In one, gently heat the milk over medium heat. Keep your eye on it to make sure it doesn't boil. In the second pot, gently melt the butter over medium-low heat. Make sure it doesn't brown. Once it's melted, take it off the heat and whisk in the flour, a little at a time, until it's incorporated and forms a smooth paste. Put the pot back on the burner over medium heat, and then add a few ladlefuls of the warm milk and start whisking everything together. When it starts to thicken, add more milk, whisking constantly, repeating the process until the sauce reaches a creamy, velvety consistency. Season with salt and pepper.

MAKES ABOUT 4 CUPS (1 L)

THE BASICS:
RICE AND RISOTTO

BOILED RICE

I make rice the same way I make pasta: I measure nothing! Here's what I do: First, I pour what I need into a fine-mesh strainer and run cold water over it a few times until the water runs clear. Then, I put it in a pot and pour in enough water to cover the rice by about 2 inches (5 cm). I bring that to a boil, then reduce the heat to a simmer and let it cook. I like my rice a bit al dente, so I start testing it for doneness a few minutes before the recommended cooking time. When it's done to my liking, I drain it.

RISOTTO BIANCO

4 cups (1 L) vegetable stock or water

3 tbsp (45 mL) extra-virgin olive oil

2 shallots or 1 medium white onion, minced

2 cups (500 mL) Italian rice (arborio, carnaroli)

1 glass dry white wine, room temperature

Salt, QB

2 tbsp (30 mL) butter

1/2 cup (125 mL) freshly grated Parmigiano-Reggiano

This is the basic template for making risotto. It has a reputation for being a long and tedious dish to prepare. Maybe that's because it needs your attention at the stove while it cooks. But it's actually a dish you can get on the table in under half an hour. And because it's all about stirring the rice over medium heat, it's a great dish to make with your kids, as long as you supervise.

Pour the stock or water into a pot and bring it to a simmer.

In a separate pan, heat the olive oil over medium heat. Add the shallots or onion and cook until they soften. Increase the heat to medium-high, add the rice and stir until all the grains of rice are coated in olive oil. Cook until the rice becomes translucent.

Add the wine, and stir, cooking until all of the liquid is absorbed. You'll smell the sweetness of the wine, and you'll start to see some of the starchy creaminess come out of the rice.

Now start to add a little warm stock or water a ladleful at a time. After every ladle goes in, you want to let it cook until the liquid is almost fully absorbed into the rice, stirring every so often to coax out the starches and to make sure nothing sticks to the pan. So add a ladle of the simmering stock and a pinch of salt, and stir. When the liquid is almost fully absorbed, add another ladleful. Keep going, ladle by ladle, until your dish looks rich and creamy, and the rice is almost, but not quite, cooked. This takes about 15 minutes.

If you're adding anything to your basic risotto, like sautéed shrimp or mushrooms, steamed mussels or puréed vegetables, now is the time to do so, so everything finishes cooking together and all the flavors can meld.

Risotto generally takes 16 to 18 minutes total. Test it by tasting it. I like mine a bit al dente. You make yours the way you like it.

The texture of the risotto can be dense and somewhat dry, or it can be "soupy." Italians say that the perfect consistency is a l'onda, which means the risotto should move like a wave when you gently shake the pot. But this is personal preference.

When you're happy with it, take it off the heat, add the butter and Parmigiano and stir well. Serve immediately.

SERVES 4 TO 6

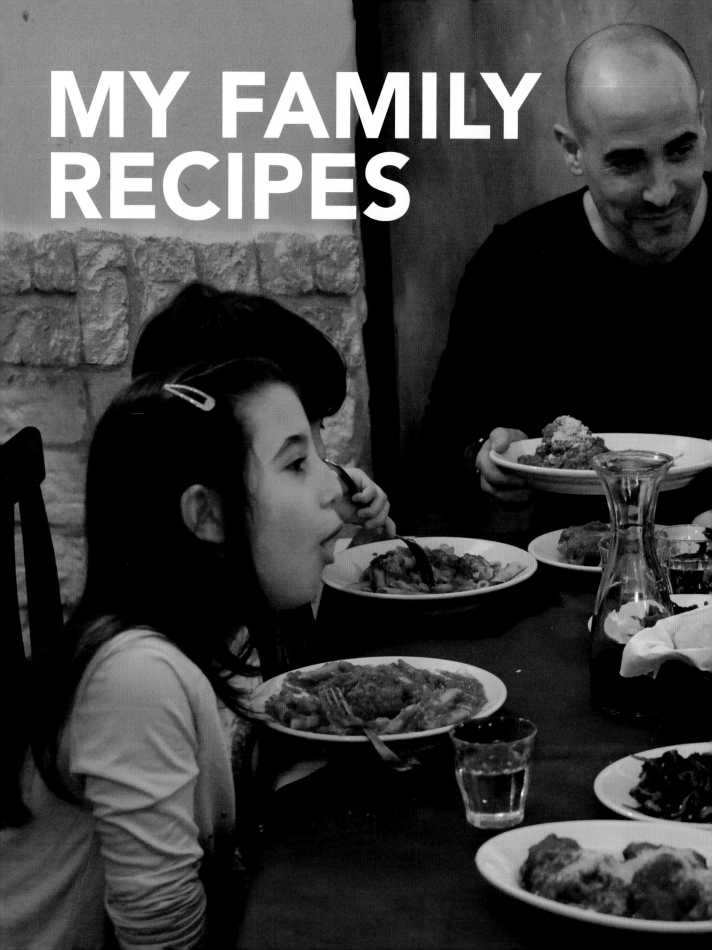

MY FAMILY RECIPES

I've always connected with food. From as far back as I remember I couldn't wait to get my hands in and start working with the ingredients. I remember the mix of excitement and frustration of being able to pour the tomato sauce into a pot, yet still being too young to turn on the stove and do my own thing.

My mom did most of the cooking, but my dad had his specialties. No matter who was running the show, my brother, sister and I were always welcome and given little jobs to do. While we cooked together, I loved hearing about how we were making dishes the same way our family had going back generations. And when we sat down to the meal, I always felt so proud of what I'd done to help make it happen.

Kitchens are magical places. When simple ingredients like flour and water come together to make pasta or bread, there's alchemy going on. But there's also alchemy in the family itself. Working together, making a meal and sitting down to share it is a very basic thing in most of our lives. And yet in my experience, even when the meal is simple, it can be a pleasure.

Now that I'm a father with three little kids, the pattern is repeating. They come into the kitchen and push their chairs up to the stove or the counter to see what they can do to help. I get them to stir the risotto, or squish tomatoes, or whatever else is safe for them to do. It's my turn to pass on the family recipes. And while I'm teaching them how to use the tools, or how the recipe has come up through the family and how to notice the magic as the ingredients come together, I get to see them learn and grow, and to relive my childhood.

RISO CON SALSA DI POMODORO

Tomato Sauce (page 19), QB

Boiled Rice (page 28), QB

Handful of freshly grated Parmigiano-Reggiano or pecorino

Extra-virgin olive oil, for drizzling

Anybody who has kids knows how crazy weeknights can be—work, school and the rest of it. This recipe is really a quick cheat, but it's worth having in your repertoire. It's delicious, and if you have a batch of cooked rice on hand, it's really fast. If you want to fancy it up, you can add some sundried tomatoes, olives and/or a tablespoon (15 mL) of pesto. The possibilities are endless. Either way, the kids will love it and it'll get you out of a weeknight bind.

Prepare or heat up the tomato sauce. When it's simmering, stir in the rice. Cook until everything is heated through. Remove it from the heat. Add a handful of Parmigiano. If you want to give it some edge, add some sharp pecorino instead. I always finish with a drizzle of olive oil.

SERVES AS MANY AS YOU LIKE

ARANCINI

4 to 5 cups (1 to 1.25 L) cooked white rice or leftover Risotto Bianco (page 29)

2 cups (500 mL) Tomato Sauce (page 19)

1 cup (250 mL) freshly grated Parmigiano-Reggiano

1/2 cup (125 mL) all-purpose flour

1 egg, beaten

1 cup (250 mL) plain dry bread crumbs

3 oz (90 g) mozzarella, cubed

Extra-virgin olive oil, for frying

To me, this is fun food, finger food. My earliest memories of arancini take me back to Italy and when my grandmother would make it for us as a snack for afternoons on the beach. It's compact, easy to eat and kid-friendly. My kids love them, and leftovers make great school lunches.

Put the rice or risotto in a bowl, then add the tomato sauce and Parmigiano and stir everything together.

You'll need three shallow dishes placed side by side. Place the flour in one dish, the beaten egg in another and the bread crumbs in the last dish.

Scoop out a handful of the rice mixture and form it into a ball. Using your thumb, make a depression in the middle of the rice ball. Place a couple of cubes of mozzarella inside, and then reshape the ball so the cheese is fully enclosed. Repeat until you have used up all of the rice. Then roll each ball first in the flour until it's lightly coated, then in the beaten egg (let any excess drip off) and finally in the bread crumbs so that it's evenly coated.

You can either panfry or deep-fry the rice balls. To panfry, fill a pan with about 1/2 inch (1 cm) of olive oil and put it over high heat. You want to heat the oil until it's very hot so the balls fry quickly and stay crisp on the outside. To see if the oil is hot enough, drop in a few bread crumbs: If the crumbs sizzle the instant they hit the oil, you're good. Working in batches so you don't crowd the pan, carefully fry a few balls at a time, turning them occasionally so they cook evenly all over. When they're golden brown, transfer them to a plate lined with paper towels to absorb excess oil.

If you are cooking the arancini in a deep fryer, preheat the oil according to the manufacturer's instructions, then gently drop the balls into the hot oil, a few at a time, and cook until golden brown all over. Transfer them to a plate lined with paper towels to absorb excess oil.

Frying the arancini gives them a crisp, golden exterior and melts the mozzarella inside. Serve warm or at room temperature.

MAKES ABOUT A DOZEN ARANCINI

COD CROQUETTES

1 lb (500 g) dried boneless skinless salt cod

2 cups (500 mL) milk

2 cloves garlic, crushed

1 large potato, peeled and boiled until tender

1 egg, beaten

1 cup (500 mL) black olives, pitted and chopped

1 tbsp (15 mL) capers, drained

1/2 cup (125 mL) finely chopped fresh flat-leaf parsley leaves

1/2 cup (125 mL) freshly grated pecorino

Salt, QB

Freshly ground black pepper, QB

1/2 cup (125 mL) or more (QB) all-purpose flour

1/2 cup (125 mL) or more (QB) plain dry bread crumbs

2 large eggs, beaten

Extra-virgin olive oil, for frying

Kids can drive you crazy with their sudden changes in taste, rejecting food they've happily eaten many times before. My mom started making these croquettes when my daughter Emma announced out of the blue that she didn't like *baccalà* (aka salt cod).

Emma loves anything with a crunchy exterior, including Arancini (see page 37), so my mom decided to make these up to look like arancini. Sure enough, Emma was super happy.

Cod croquettes are one of those dishes that are sophisticated enough for parents but also make a good snack or light dinner for kids (if your kids don't already eat fish, this is an easy way to introduce them to it). Think of these as a fancier version of fish sticks. These are also easy to make—it just takes some planning, because you need to soak the salt cod for 24 hours.

This is one of those dishes that you make your own. I'm giving you some basic quantities to get you started, but this is truly a QB recipe. Add as much of the olives, capers, parsley and cheese as you like.

Put the cod in a large bowl and cover it with cold water. Leave it in the fridge for 24 hours, changing the water three to four times to get rid of the salt and soften up the fish. After 24 hours, drain the fish and cut it into small chunks.

Pour the milk into a pot, add the garlic and bring it to a simmer over medium-high heat. Add the cod pieces and cook for 10 minutes. Drain the cod and set it aside until cool enough to handle. When cool, squeeze out any excess liquid. Put the cod in a mixing bowl and, using a fork, break it into smaller pieces.

Using a potato ricer, rice the potato so it's fluffy. (If you don't have a ricer, mash the potatoes with a fork.) Add it to the cod, along with the beaten egg, olives, capers, parsley, pecorino and salt and pepper. Mix well.

You'll need three shallow dishes placed side by side. Place the flour in one dish, the 2 large beaten eggs in another and the bread crumbs in the last dish.

With your hands, scoop up some of the cod mixture and roll it into a ball slightly bigger than a golf ball. Repeat until all of the cod mixture is used up. Roll each ball first in the flour until lightly coated, then in the beaten eggs (let any excess drip off) and finally in the bread crumbs.

To fry the croquettes: Pour 1/2 to 1 inch (1 cm to 2.5 cm) of olive oil into a frying pan. You want to heat the oil until very hot so the balls fry quickly. To see if the oil is hot enough, drop in a few bread crumbs: If the crumbs sizzle the instant they hit the oil, you're good. Working in batches so you don't crowd the pan, carefully fry a few balls at a time, turning them occasionally so they cook evenly all over. Transfer them to a plate covered with paper towels to absorb excess oil. Serve warm or at room temperature. They should never be eaten piping hot.

MAKES ABOUT 20 CROQUETTES

MUSSELS AND MOZZARELLA STICKS

24 mussels, bearded, steamed and shells discarded

1 mozzarella ball (8 oz/250 g), cut into 24 cubes

1/2 cup (125 mL) all-purpose flour

1 large egg

1/2 cup (125 mL) plain dry bread crumbs

Salt, QB

Freshly ground black pepper, QB

Extra-virgin olive oil, for frying

I picked up these next two recipes on the Amalfi Coast. They're delicious snacks that are crunchy and full of flavor. For some people it's a huge no-no to mix seafood and cheese. But because you're using a delicate-flavored creamy mozzarella, the cheese complements rather than obliterates the fish. This is great finger food for a cocktail party or a picnic. Everyone loves them. My kids go nuts for them.

Using a toothpick, skewer a mussel, followed by a cube of mozzarella, then repeat. You should be able to fit two of each per toothpick. Repeat with the remaining mussels and mozzarella cubes.

Put the flour, the beaten egg, and the bread crumbs on separate plates. Add a little salt and pepper to the bread crumbs and mix to combine.

Dredge each skewer first in the flour, then dip in the beaten egg, letting any excess drip off, and roll in the bread crumbs until completely covered.

Pour about 1/2 inch (1 cm) of olive oil into a frying pan and put it over high heat. When the oil is hot, carefully place the skewers in it. Fry until golden brown, turning as needed.

Transfer the cooked skewers to a plate lined with paper towels to absorb excess oil. Serve warm or at room temperature.

MAKES 12 STICKS

ANCHOVIES IN LOVE

1 lb (500 g) large fresh anchovies

Flour for dredging

3 1/2 oz (100 g) *prosciutto cotto* or cooked ham, thinly sliced

1 ball mozzarella di bufala (buffalo mozzarella), thinly sliced

1/2 cup (125 mL) all-purpose flour

1 large egg, beaten

1/2 cup (125 mL) plain dry bread crumbs

Salt, QB

Freshly ground black pepper, QB

Extra-virgin olive oil, for frying

This is a simple assembly job, so don't let the fact that you have to clean the anchovies throw you. It's really easy.

To clean the anchovies: With your fingers, rip off the head. Then pull the anchovy open like a little book, take out the spine, and give the fillet a quick rinse under cold running water. Dredge the fillet in flour, shake off any excess and lay on a plate, skin-side down. Repeat with the remaining anchovies.

Top half of the fillets with a slice of *prosciutto cotto* or ham and a slice of mozzarella. Then cover with a second anchovy fillet, skin-side up, so that you've made a little sandwich.

Put the flour, the beaten egg and the bread crumbs on separate plates. Add salt and pepper to the bread crumbs and mix to combine.

Now take each little fillet sandwich, dip it in the beaten egg and then roll it in bread crumbs so that it's well coated.

Pour about 1/2 inch (1 cm) of olive oil into a frying pan set over high heat. You want the oil hot so the little sandwiches fry quickly. Carefully drop the anchovy sandwiches in the hot oil a few at a time and fry until they're golden brown. These will cook quickly, so keep your eyes on them. Transfer them to a plate lined with paper towels to absorb excess oil. Serve warm or at room temperature.

SERVES 6

ZUCCHINI AND ONION FRITTATA

8 large eggs, well beaten

1 cup (250 mL) freshly grated Parmigiano-Reggiano

Salt, QB

Freshly ground black pepper, QB

Fresh mint, finely chopped, QB

Extra-virgin olive oil, for frying

1 onion, thinly sliced

2 zucchini, thinly sliced

Frittatas are a gift to busy families. They're like a quiche without a crust or an omelet but with a bit more substance. You can serve them immediately or make them ahead, put them in the fridge and send your kids to school with sliced frittata in a *panino*. You can also easily substitute the ingredients for whatever you have on hand, using your favorite combination of flavors. This is mine.

In a bowl, whisk together the eggs and Parmigiano with a little salt and pepper and the mint. Because you're adding a good amount of cheese, you might want to go easy on the salt.

Heat up a frying pan over medium-high to high heat and add some olive oil. When the oil shimmers, add the onion and zucchini and cook until they get a little golden. Reduce the heat slightly, then pour in the beaten egg mixture so that it covers the onion and zucchini evenly.

Once the frittata is mostly set but the middle is still a bit wet-looking, you can do one of two things: You can go old-school, the way I saw my grandmother do it, and rest an oversized plate on the top of the frying pan, which will trap in all the steam and cook the top. Or you can turn the broiler on and let the pan sit in the oven for a few minutes, until the frittata is set but not overcooked.

Serve warm or cold.

SERVES 4

FRITTATA DI PASTA

Eggs, QB

Salt, QB

Freshly grated Parmigiano-Reggiano, QB (optional)

Leftover cooked pasta, QB

Extra-virgin olive oil, QB

When I was a kid the kind of food we ate was one of the big things that differentiated us, the Italians, from the neighbors. I went through a dark period when I just wanted to eat what everyone else was eating, no matter how bland or boring it might be. But then that changed.

This might be the recipe that swung schoolyard opinion in my favor. To this day my non-Italian friends die for this dish, and everyone who tries it says it is the best! We make it for our kids to take to school. Inevitably they come home and tell us, "Everyone loves this, so can you make extra—the other kids want some, too."

Just a note: You can use any kind of leftover pasta and sauce you have on hand. I've made this with spaghetti, fusilli—really any short or long pasta with sauce that you have left over. It always tastes delicious, so I strongly recommend that if you make pasta, make extra. With this recipe in your back pocket, leftovers will never go to waste. It also makes great beach or picnic food.

The quantities of eggs and cheese will depend on how much pasta you have left over, so I have just given you the ingredients and you can judge for yourself when you are making it. Just make sure that you use enough eggs to coat the noodles completely. I recommend using a non-stick pan, if you have one.

In a large mixing bowl, beat the eggs. Add a bit of salt—but just a bit, because the pasta already has flavor. If you want, you can add a handful of Parmigiano and stir it in. Then add the pasta and mix it well so that it is fully coated in the egg mixture.

In a large frying pan, heat up a good amount of olive oil over high heat. When the oil shimmers, pour in the pasta mixture, flattening it out evenly in your pan. Cook it for about 5 minutes, until the bottom gets golden brown and crisp. Then flip it over: Cover the pan with a large plate and then carefully flip them together so the fried pasta falls onto the plate. Place the pan back on the stove, then slide the pasta back into the pan, browned-side up, and cook until golden brown.

Let the frittata cool down before serving—it always tastes better at room temperature.

SERVES AS MANY AS YOU LIKE

PAPPA AL POMODORO

1/2 cup (125 mL) extra-virgin olive oil

1 stalk celery, finely chopped

1 carrot, finely chopped

1 small onion, finely chopped

1 loaf stale Tuscan-style or dense country-style bread, cut into small pieces

1 to 2 cups (250 to 500 mL) vegetable stock

Salt, QB

Freshly ground black pepper, QB

2 cans (19 oz/540 mL) whole plum tomatoes, with juices

Your best extra-virgin olive oil, for drizzling, QB

5 fresh basil leaves (or QB), whole or roughly torn

The word *pappa* means "mush," as in the kind of food you'd feed a baby. In the case of Pappa al Pomodoro, it refers to the texture of the finished dish, which is soft, silky and mushy, kind of like baby food.

This is classic *cucina povera* (peasant cooking), created back in the day by Tuscan farmers who had stale bread they needed to use up. It's so humble and yet incredibly delicious. In fact, when I serve this to my non-Italian friends they're always shocked at how good it is and how easy it is to make. It's also a great dish to make with your kids. I get mine to rip up the bread and squish the tomatoes with their hands. What kid wouldn't love to do that?

Even though this has humble beginnings, don't be fooled. Those Tuscan peasant farmers had amazing olive oil. So use the best you can to drizzle over at the end. I tend to make this a lot in the fall when I can get my hands on the newly pressed olive oil.

Heat 1/2 cup (125 mL) of olive oil in a large pot over medium heat. Add the celery, carrot and onion and sauté them until they soften and start to turn golden. Add the bread and stir until all the pieces are coated in olive oil. Add a few ladlefuls of vegetable stock and stir. Keep adding the vegetable stock a couple of ladlefuls at a time, stirring after each addition. Season with salt and pepper as you go. The bread will start to break down and form the *pappa*. You can stop when you get to the *pappa* texture or add more stock to make it soupier.

Add the plum tomatoes. If the tomatoes aren't squished beforehand, break them up right in the pot using the back of the spoon. Let the mixture simmer, uncovered, over low heat for about half an hour.

Turn off the heat, cover and let sit for a few hours to let the flavors come together and intensify. Serve warm (not hot!) or at room temperature.

Just before serving, hit it with a good drizzle of your very best extra-virgin olive oil and the basil.

SERVES 4 TO 6

RIBOLLITA

Extra-virgin olive oil, QB

1 small onion, chopped

1 clove garlic, finely chopped

1 large stalk celery, chopped

1 large carrot, chopped

1 potato, peeled and chopped

1/2 head savoy cabbage, thinly sliced

1/2 head *cavalo nero* (black cabbage), thinly sliced

1 bunch kale, roughly chopped

Salt, QB

Freshly ground black pepper, QB

2 cups (500 mL) cooked borlotti beans (romano beans) or 1 can (19 oz/540 mL) borlotti beans, rinsed and drained

1 can (28 oz/796 mL) whole peeled plum tomatoes, with juices

2 to 3 cups (500 to 750 mL) vegetable stock

6 slices country bread, torn into pieces

This is another classic Italian soup that comes from *cucina povera*. The name means "reboiled," and its origins are, again, in a dish created to use up stale bread, leftovers or vegetables that were going bad, so what went into it would always change. I tend to make it differently each time, but the constants are bread, beans, tomatoes and greens. I love this style of soup, especially on cold winter nights.

Heat some olive oil in a large soup pot over medium-high heat. Add the onion, garlic, celery and carrot and sauté until soft. Add the potato, savoy cabbage, *cavalo nero*, kale and some salt and pepper and stir. Cook until the greens start to wilt.

Now add the beans and, using the back of a wooden spoon, mash up some of them for a bit of texture and creaminess.

Add the tomatoes. You can either put the tomatoes in a bowl and squeeze them with your hands to break them up before you put them in, or you can mash them right in the pot with the back of the wooden spoon. Then add the stock and bread. Reduce the heat and let everything simmer for about 45 minutes to an hour, until the bread softens and breaks up. The bread will help the soup achieve a nice, thick *pappa*-like texture. Add more salt and pepper to taste.

Turn off the heat and let the ribollita sit for an hour so the flavors come together. I eat it at room temperature. Finish each serving with a drizzle of really good extra-virgin olive oil.

SERVES 4 TO 6

CALAMARI AND CHICKPEA PASTA

1 lb (500 g) fresh squid

1 lb (500 g) tubetti or ditalini pasta

Extra-virgin olive oil, QB. Plus extra for drizzling

1 small onion, finely chopped

1 tsp (5 mL) dried chili flakes

1 cup (250 mL) cherry tomatoes, quartered

2 cups (500 mL) cooked chickpeas (page 10) or 1 can (19 oz/540 mL) chickpeas, rinsed and drained

1 small bunch fresh flat-leaf parsley, chopped

1/2 cup (125 mL) dry white wine

Salt, QB

Freshly ground black pepper, QB

1 tbsp (15 mL) Pesto Genovese (page 25) or QB

Freshly grated Parmigiano-Reggiano, QB

My dad loves *ceci e pasta*, or chickpea and pasta soup. One day I made this spin on that classic and he went crazy for it, so now I make it for him all the time. This recipe calls for squid, but I've also made it with mussels and clams when I can't get fresh squid, and it's equally delicious.

To start, give the squid a good rinse inside and out, then cut the bodies into medium-size rings and finely chop the tentacles.

Get your sauce and your pasta going at the same time.

Put a large pot of water on to boil. When the water boils, salt it and drop in the pasta. Give it a quick stir.

In another pot, heat some olive oil over medium heat and sauté the onion. Just before the onion softens, stir in the chili flakes. Let it cook until the onion becomes soft, sweet and translucent.

Add the tomatoes, chickpeas and parsley and cook for about 5 minutes, stirring every so often, until the tomatoes start to soften and lose their shape. Add the squid and toss with the other ingredients. Then stir in the wine and cook for a minute or two until it reduces a little. At this point I like to mash up some of the chickpeas to give the dish a thicker, creamier texture.

When your pasta is al dente, drain it, reserving 1/2 to 1 cup (125 to 250 mL) of the pasta cooking water.

Add the cooked pasta to the pan with the pesto. Stir in just enough of the reserved pasta cooking water to get the consistency you like. Let everything cook for a few minutes so the flavors come together. Taste and adjust the seasonings. To finish, sprinkle with some Parmigiano and a drizzle of olive oil.

Serve immediately.

SERVES 4 TO 6

CHICKEN AND PRICKLY PEAR SALAD

1 prickly pear per person

Mixed fresh salad greens, QB

Extra-virgin olive oil, QB

Balsamic vinegar, QB

Salt, QB

Freshly ground black pepper, QB

Cooked chicken, sliced, QB

Toasted almonds, roughly chopped, QB

I hated prickly pears (cactus fruit) when I was growing up. I was never really a fussy eater, but whenever I saw a plate of prickly pears coming to the table I would wince. When you're a kid, a fruit that seems to be full of little stones is off-putting. In our house you ate what the adults ate, so it wasn't going to go away. I gradually got used to it, and now I have a weird affinity for it. I love its sweetness and unique texture. Oh, how we grow up to become our parents!

This is a simple salad. I love the combination of leafy greens, meat and fruit. It's a great way to use up leftover chicken—grilled, poached, seared, roasted.

First peel the prickly pear. True to its name, the skin is covered in little thorns, so be careful. Stick a fork in the side of the fruit so you can hold it steady, and use a very sharp knife to cut off the ends. To peel the fruit, still holding it with the fork, make a shallow cut through the skin lengthwise from end to end. Then insert the knife between the skin and the flesh and pull the skin back. Once you get going, this will be easy. At some point you'll be able to simply lift the flesh away from the peel. Cut the peeled fruit into even slices and set aside.

Put your mixed greens in a large bowl and drizzle with olive oil and a light hit of balsamic. Season with salt and pepper and toss until the greens are well coated. Arrange the greens on a serving plate and top with slices of chicken and prickly pear. To finish, sprinkle with toasted almonds.

SERVES AS MANY AS YOU LIKE

PORCINI SALTATI

6 fresh porcini mushrooms

1/4 cup (60 mL) extra-virgin olive oil, plus more for drizzling

2 cloves garlic, finely chopped

2 sprigs fresh nepitella, or a combination of equal parts chopped fresh mint and fresh oregano, or chopped fresh flat-leaf parsley, QB

Salt, QB

Freshly ground black pepper, QB

Whipping (35%) cream, QB (optional)

Porcini are the king of Italian mushrooms. They have a meaty yet soft and silky texture, and they make anything you pair them with taste even better by association. For busy families—busy anyone, really—Porcini Saltati is a great dish to have in your repertoire. You can put it on crostini, serve it with some grilled chicken or use it in a risotto.

There are dried porcini and fresh porcini. The dried are good for things like risotto. For this recipe, use only fresh.

When you buy porcini in Tuscany, the vendor will give you a little bouquet of a wild herb called nepitella to cook with the mushrooms. If you can't get nepitella but want that Tuscan flavor, substitute equal parts chopped fresh mint and oregano. You can also just use fresh parsley. Each herb has its merits, and each will give the dish a different spin.

Never wash porcini. Clean them by wiping the dirt off with a towel. Use a paring knife to gently scape off any stubborn bits of dirt that remain and trim off the bottoms of the stems. Then roughly chop them and set aside.

Heat the olive oil in a frying pan over medium heat. When the oil shimmers, add the garlic and cook for 20 to 30 seconds. Add the chopped porcini and sauté for about 5 minutes. Add the herbs and salt and pepper, and cook for another few minutes, until the mushrooms are soft, silky and cooked through. Then turn off the stove.

To serve this with crostini: Toast your sliced bread, rub all over with a clove of garlic and spoon the porcini saltati on top.

To make a cream sauce: After you've added the herbs, salt and pepper, pour in a little cream, turn the heat up to high and cook until the cream thickens up and starts to bubble. Serve immediately.

SERVES 4

PORCINI RISOTTO

4 cups (1 L) vegetable stock

1/4 cup (60 mL) extra-virgin olive oil

2 medium shallots, finely diced

Handful of dried porcini mushrooms

2 cups (500 mL) arborio rice

1 cup (250 mL) dry white wine

1 batch Porcini Saltati (page 65)

1 tbsp (15 mL) butter

Freshly grated Parmigiano-Reggiano, QB

This is a deeply satisfying risotto, thanks to the addition of porcini mushrooms. Their meaty texture and earthy flavor is a perfect marriage with the creamy rice. This recipe uses both fresh and dried porcini for extra intensity of flavor.

Pour the vegetable stock into a saucepan and bring it to a simmer.

In a large pot, heat the olive oil over medium-high heat. Add the shallots and cook, stirring every so often, until they become translucent. Crumble in a handful of the dried porcini and add the rice, stirring to coat each grain with the oil. Cook, stirring occasionally, until the rice becomes translucent. Add the white wine and cook until it is absorbed by the rice.

Now start to add a little warm stock a ladleful at a time. After every ladle goes in, you want to let it cook until the liquid is almost fully absorbed into the rice, stirring every so often to coax out the starches from the rice and to make sure it doesn't stick. Keep going this way until the stock is used up and the rice is almost cooked, 15 to 16 minutes.

Stir in the Porcini Saltati, and cook for another 1 to 2 minutes. Taste to make sure you're happy with the way the rice is seasoned and cooked. I like a little bite to mine, but I leave that up to you. The whole process takes 16 to 18 minutes.

Take it off the heat and stir in the butter and the Parmigiano. Serve immediately.

SERVES 4 TO 6

CACIO E PEPE CON PECORINO "GELATO"

Pecorino Gelato

2 cups (500 mL) heavy cream

Pinch of salt

1 cup (250 mL) freshly grated pecorino

Cacio e Pepe

1 lb (500 g) short fresh pasta (your choice)

2 tbsp (30 mL) extra-virgin olive oil, plus more for drizzling

2 tbsp (30 mL) black peppercorns (a mix of fine and coarse ground)

1/2 cup (125 mL) freshly grated pecorino

Freshly cracked black pepper, to finish

This is a spin on one of my favorite dishes, the classic Cacio e Pepe. I came up with this version when I was in Florence. One day I had lunch with my friend Vitulio Bondi, who is the president of the Traditional Gelato Association of Florence. He also has his own *gelateria* and a school. We were talking about the trends in savory gelatos and did a tasting of some of his latest flavors. It inspired me to go home and try something out of the box.

Now, the classic recipe has just three ingredients: pasta, cheese and pepper. But, instead of putting the cheese in the pasta, I thought, why not make it into a "gelato" and add that to the pasta? It was really fantastic. I love the way the gelato melts into the hot pasta, creating something fun and unexpected.

To make the pecorino gelato: In a heavy-bottomed pot over medium heat, heat the cream. Add a pinch of salt. When the cream starts to bubble, reduce the heat and add the pecorino a little at time, whisking until melted. When all the cheese has been incorporated, remove the pan from the heat. Pour your mixture through a fine-mesh sieve onto a metal tray. Let it cool, then cover it with the plastic wrap and put it in the freezer for about 2 hours.

To make the cacio e pepe: Put a large pot of water on to boil. When the water boils, salt it and drop in the pasta. Fresh pasta cooks quickly and will rise to the surface in 2 to 3 minutes, which means it's ready.

While your pasta is cooking, pour the olive oil into a small frying pan over low heat. Add your mix of ground pepper and cook for 2 to 3 minutes, shaking the pan every so often, until the black pepper becomes lightly fragrant. Increase the heat to medium-low and then, if you want, add in about half a ladleful of pasta water and let that cook for 30 seconds or so.

When the pasta is al dente, drain it, reserving about 1 cup (250 mL) of the pasta cooking water. Add the pasta to the frying pan and toss to coat.

Add the pecorino, a little at a time, tossing your pasta until it's completely coated, creamy and flecked with the pepper. If the sauce is too thick, add a little bit more of the reserved pasta water to loosen it up.

Serve immediately with a scoop of pecorino gelato on top, along with some freshly cracked black pepper and a drizzle of olive oil.

SERVES 4 TO 6

CAVATELLI

2 cups (500 mL) fine semolina flour

1 cup (250 mL) all-purpose flour, plus more for dusting

1/2 tsp (2 mL) salt

1 cup (250 mL) warm water

Cavatelli is a rustic, Southern-style *pasta fresca* that I really love. It's easy to make. You don't need a pasta maker, and it's hearty enough to stand up to earthy sauces. It works really well with Ragù Napoletano (page 20). This is a basic cavatelli recipe, followed by a few other sauces that work really well with it.

To make the dough: Pour the flours into a big bowl. In another bowl, add the salt to the water and stir until the salt is completely dissolved. Gradually pour the salted water into the flours, mixing it with your hands until the flour has absorbed as much water as possible and starts to form a dough. Now turn the dough out onto a lightly floured work surface and begin to knead. Be patient. Resist the urge to add more water. For the next 5 minutes or so, you have to knead the dough, continuing to incorporate the flour, until it comes together and forms a smooth, soft ball. Wrap it in plastic wrap and let it rest at room temperature for half an hour.

To make the cavatelli: Divide the ball of dough into four equal portions. Working with one portion at a time, roll the dough out with a rolling pin as you would a pizza, until it's about 1/4 inch (0.5 cm) thick. Using a sharp knife, cut the rolled-out dough into 1/2-inch (1 cm) strips. Then cut each of those strips into 1/2-inch (1 cm) pieces. Using your fingertips, gently but firmly press down and pull back on each little dough square. The piece of pasta will curl, and that's your cavatelli noodle. Every one is going to have its own personality and shape, and that's part of the charm of this dish.

Because this is fresh pasta, it will cook very quickly. Put the cavatelli in a pot of boiling salted water and give it a gentle stir. When they rise to the surface in 2 to 3 minutes, they're ready to be drained and added to your sauce.

Note: Fresh cavatelli freeze well. To freeze, lay them out on a baking sheet lined with parchment paper. When they're frozen, put them into freezer bags. Use within 3 to 4 months. You can cook them directly from frozen.

MAKES 1 LB (500 G) CAVATELLI

CAVATELLI WITH CHERRY TOMATOES AND PANCETTA

1/4 cup (60 mL) extra-virgin olive oil

1 medium red onion, thinly sliced

2 cloves garlic, crushed

5 oz (150 g) pancetta, cubed

1 pint (25 to 30) cherry tomatoes

1/4 cup (60 mL) dry white wine

1 batch (500 g) Cavatelli (page 70)

Salt, QB

1/2 cup (125 mL) freshly grated Parmigiano-Reggiano

1 bunch arugula, chopped

This is a very simple sauce that works really well with fresh cavatelli or any short pasta, fresh or dried.

Start making your sauce and pasta at the same time. Put a large pot of water on to boil.

Heat the olive oil in a large skillet over medium-high heat. When the oil shimmers, add the onion, garlic and pancetta and cook, stirring occasionally, until the onion is translucent. Stir in the tomatoes and cook until they soften and begin to break down. Add in the white wine and stir to pick up any bits on the bottom of the pan. This will pull even more flavor into your sauce. The alcohol will evaporate and give the sauce a lovely sweetness. At that point, remove the pan from the heat and set aside.

Add your cavatelli to the boiling water, along with some salt, and give it a gentle stir. Cook the pasta for 2 to 3 minutes, until they rise to the surface. Drain, reserving about 1/2 cup (125 mL) of the cooking water.

Add the cooked pasta to your pan of sauce along with some of the reserved pasta cooking water to loosen up the sauce. Toss it all together. Put it back over medium-high heat and cook, stirring gently, just to heat it through, about 30 seconds. Remove the pan from the heat. Top with freshly grated Parmigiano and chopped arugula.

Serve immediately.

SERVES 4

CAVATELLI WITH SAUSAGE, FENNEL AND CHANTERELLES

1 batch (500 g) Cavatelli (page 70)

3 tbsp (45 mL) extra-virgin olive oil

3 cloves garlic, smashed

1/2 tsp (2 mL) dried chili flakes

9 oz (275 g) spicy sausage, casings removed

Salt, QB

1 lb (500 g) fresh chanterelles or other wild mushrooms, trimmed and torn into pieces

1 bunch fennel fronds, chopped (reserve one-third for garnish)

1/2 cup (125 mL) freshly grated Parmigiano-Reggiano

I love the earthy combination of sausage, fennel and chanterelle mushrooms. It works really well with hearty cavatelli pasta. You can also make this using any short pasta, fresh or dried.

Put a large pot of water on to boil. When the water boils, salt it and drop in the pasta. Give it a gentle stir. Because the pasta is fresh, it will take only 2 to 3 minutes to cook. It will rise to the top when it's done. Drain the pasta, reserving 1/2 cup (125 mL) of the pasta cooking water.

In a large frying pan, heat the olive oil over medium-high heat. Add the garlic and chili flakes and sauté for about 30 seconds. Then crumble in the sausage and cook, stirring occasionally, until the meat is about halfway cooked. Add a pinch of salt and the mushrooms, and continue cooking until both the meat and the mushrooms are done. Remove and discard the garlic cloves. Toss in the fennel fronds and give it all a stir.

Add your cooked pasta, along with some of the reserved pasta cooking water, to the sauce. Toss to combine and cook for another 20 to 30 seconds to let the flavors come together. Remove the pan from the heat, add the Parmigiano and give the whole thing another toss.

Serve immediately, garnishing each serving with fresh fennel fronds.

SERVES 4

FUSILLI CON TONNO E PISTACCHI

1 lb (500 g) fusilli pasta

Extra-virgin olive oil, QB

1 small red onion, finely chopped

2 cans (5 oz/150 g) good-quality tuna packed in oil, drained

1 cup (250 mL) shelled unsalted pistachios, roughly chopped

1 bunch fennel fronds, chopped

I came up with this dish one day when I was hanging out with my nephew Giovanni. He was telling me about his vacation in Sicily and how much he loved the food. So, I was inspired to make this for him based on some of the ingredients I associate with Sicily. Wild fennel grows all over the place there, and Sicilians use a lot of it when they cook, especially in their seafood. Some of the best pistachios in the world come from Bronte in Sicily. And I love the way they both work with tuna. Because neither the fennel nor pistachios are really cooked in this dish, make sure they're fresh.

Start making your sauce and pasta at the same time.

Put a large pot of water on to boil. When the water boils, salt it and drop in the pasta.

Heat the olive oil in a sauté pan over medium heat. When the oil shimmers, add the onion and let it cook slowly until translucent. Add the tuna and stir well. Remove the pan from the heat. To the pan, add three-quarters of the pistachio and three-quarters of the fennel fronds, and stir everything together.

Drain the pasta just before it is al dente, reserving about 1/2 cup (125 mL) of the cooking water.

Add the cooked pasta, along with some of the reserved cooking water, to your tuna and onion mixture. Toss everything together for about 30 seconds to let the flavors come together.

Serve immediately, garnishing each plate with some of the remaining pistachios and fennel fronds.

SERVES 4

MY CAULIFLOWER PUTTANESCA PASTA

1/4 cup (60 mL) extra-virgin olive oil, plus more for drizzling

1 medium white onion, diced

6 anchovy fillets, roughly chopped

1 cup (250 mL) black olives, pitted

2 tbsp (30 mL) capers, drained

1/2 tsp (2 mL) dried chili flakes

1 can (28 oz/796 mL) crushed tomatoes

1 head cauliflower, cut into small florets

1 lb (500 g) pasta

1/2 cup (125 mL) freshly grated Parmigiano-Reggiano

1/2 cup (125 mL) freshly grated pecorino

I generally find cauliflower to be a very bland vegetable, so I like to use it in dishes that contrast that blandness with sharp-flavored ingredients like anchovies and capers. Put that over pasta and you have a really interesting mix of tastes and textures. This is a hearty one-pot, family-style meal.

Heat the olive oil in a large sauté pan or pot over medium-high heat. When the oil shimmers, add the onion, anchovies, olives and capers and sauté for a few minutes until the anchovies start to dissolve and the onion starts to soften. Stir in the chili flakes and tomatoes, then add the cauliflower. Cook for half an hour, stirring occasionally to make sure that nothing sticks, or until the cauliflower is tender.

Once the cauliflower is ready, put a large pot of water on to boil. When the water boils, salt it and drop in the pasta. As soon as it's about two-thirds of the way cooked, drain the pasta, reserving 1 to 2 cups (250 to 500 mL) of the cooking water.

Transfer the pasta to the sauce along with some of the reserved pasta cooking water. Turn off the heat. Top with the cheeses and drizzle with some olive oil. Give everything a stir and then let it rest for 5 minutes so all the flavors can come together.

SERVES 6

SPAGHETTI WITH BABY OCTOPUS

1/4 cup (60 mL) extra-virgin olive oil

2 cloves garlic, crushed

Dried chili flakes, QB

6 whole baby octopus, cleaned

1 cup (250 mL) dry white wine

3 cups (750 mL) passata

Salt, QB

1 lb (500 g) spaghettoni pasta (thick spaghetti)

Fresh flat-leaf parsley, chopped, QB

This is a beautiful slow-cooked ragù-style pasta sauce, but instead of meat, you're using baby octopus. The tomato sauce takes on the flavor of the octopus and, just like a meat ragù, you end up with both a sauce for your pasta and a separate dish for your *secondo*.

This spaghetti was a Rocco Christmas standard, so for me, no matter when I have it, it is happy food. It takes me back to those family celebrations.

Heat the olive oil in a large sauté pan or pot over medium heat. Add the garlic, chili flakes and baby octopus. Sauté for a minute or so, then add the white wine and cook until it is reduced by two-thirds. Add the passata and salt. Bring the mixture to a light boil, then reduce the heat and let it simmer for 3 hours. The octopus will be tender. What I like to do when I serve it is remove all but one or two octopus from the sauce. I break up the remaining ones a bit to create texture.

Put a large pot of water on to boil. When the water boils, salt it and drop in the pasta. Cook until just before it is al dente. Drain the pasta, reserving about 1/2 cup (125 mL) of the cooking water.

Add the cooked pasta to the sauce, along with some chopped parsley and the reserved pasta cooking water, and let it finish cooking until it's al dente.

You can then serve the pasta on its own, with the reserved octopus as a *secondo*, or you can serve it all together.

SERVES 4

OCTOPUS AND BEANS

1 to 2 lb (500 g to 1 kg) fresh octopus

1/2 cup (125 mL) extra-virgin olive oil

1 cup (250 mL) cherry tomatoes

1 zucchini or 1 stalk celery

1 bunch fresh flat-leaf parsley, chopped

2 cups (500 mL) cooked cannellini beans (page 10) or 1 can (19 oz/540 mL) cannellini beans, rinsed and drained

Juice of 1 lemon

Salt, QB

Freshly cracked black pepper, QB

I love octopus, pretty much any way it's cooked. And octopus and beans is a combination that works really well served warm or cold. You can either grill the octopus after it's been boiled or simply cool the boiled octopus and serve it as a salad. I like both versions—it all depends on the mood I'm in! Use this recipe as inspiration.

I know a lot of people who like octopus but are freaked out by the idea of preparing it. They'll order it at a restaurant, but won't work with it at home. Trust me, cleaning octopus is not that big of a deal. This is how you do it: First rinse the octopus well under cold running water, making sure you get rid of any grit. Flip it over and look for the beak on the underside, which is the hard, shell-like bit in the middle. Just cut it out with a knife.

Put the octopus in a large pot with enough cold water to cover it and bring it to a boil. You don't have to salt the water because the octopus is salty enough. When the water comes to a boil, reduce the heat to medium and let the octopus simmer for about an hour, until it's fork-tender. In my family, we throw a wine cork in the cooking water, because there is a school of thought that says enzymes from the cork help to tenderize the octopus.

Drain the cooked octopus and set it aside until it is cool enough to handle. Using a sharp knife, cut off the head and discard it. At this point you can either cut the tentacles into bite-size pieces and proceed with the recipe or you can char the whole tentacles on the grill first and then cut them into bite-size pieces. It's up to you.

To serve this dish warm: Heat up a frying pan over medium-low heat. Add the olive oil, then the tomatoes, zucchini or celery, parsley and beans and cook until the flavors marry and everything is heated through. Then add the chopped cooked octopus and lemon juice, toss everything together and cook for another minute or so, just to warm the octopus. Season with salt and pepper, and serve immediately.

To serve this dish as a salad: In a mixing bowl, combine the tomatoes, zucchini or celery, parsley, beans and cooked octopus. Season with the olive oil, lemon juice and salt and pepper. Serve.

SERVES 4 TO 6

STEWED CUTTLEFISH AND SPINACH

1 to 1 1/2 lb (500 to 750 g) cuttlefish, cleaned

1/4 cup (60 mL) extra-virgin olive oil

3 cloves garlic, finely chopped

Dried chili flakes, QB

4 anchovy fillets, finely chopped

2 tbsp (30 mL) capers, drained

1 cup (250 mL) dry white wine

2 cups (500 mL) passata

1 cup (250 mL) canned diced tomatoes, with juices

1 bunch fresh spinach, trimmed and chopped

Salt, QB

Grilled bread rubbed with garlic and drizzled with olive oil, for serving

The first time my kids ate this dish, I told them the cuttlefish was chicken. Sometimes as parents, you have to do what you have to do. You see, while I was making dinner they were watching a cartoon that featured charming sea creatures as characters. It seemed like lying was the kinder option. But then in my defense, the kids loved it. So the next time I served it, I told them what it really was, and I made sure they weren't watching cartoons before dinner.

Just a note: If you can't find cuttlefish, you can use squid. Cuttlefish is a little meatier, though, and holds up well to long, slow cooking.

Cut the cuttlefish into thin strips and pieces. Set aside.

Heat up the olive oil in a pot over medium heat. Add the garlic, chili flakes, anchovies and capers and cook, stirring, for a minute or so. Don't let the garlic burn. Add the cuttlefish and cook until the flesh turns white, about 5 minutes. Add the wine, increase the heat to medium-high and cook until the liquid has reduced by about half. Stir in the passata and diced tomatoes, and add a bit of salt, but not too much at this point (you can taste and adjust the seasonings when the dish is almost done).

Reduce the heat to medium and stir the mixture well. Cover with a lid and let cook for 20 minutes. Add the spinach and cook for another 20 minutes, stirring occasionally. Once it's done, remove the pot from the heat and let it rest, covered, for an hour.

Serve with thick slices of grilled bread rubbed with a clove of garlic and a drizzle of olive oil. Make lots of it because this dish is so good you'll want to use the bread to mop up any sauce left on your plate—or as Italians call this, *scarpetta*.

SERVES 4 TO 6

PIZZAIOLA SAUCE

1/4 cup (60 mL) extra-virgin olive oil

1 clove garlic, thinly sliced

Dried chili flakes, QB (optional)

6 cherry tomatoes, quartered

2 cups (500 mL) passata, divided

1 tbsp (15 mL) tomato paste

1 tsp (5 mL) dried oregano

Salt, QB

Fresh basil, QB

The Pignasecca street market is a small outdoor market in Naples. I was staying in the area and no matter where I was going, I always cut through the market. Every day I'd see a woman who was selling three ingredients: oregano, garlic and chili. With true Neapolitan charm and spirit she'd be yelling at the people walking by to pick up a deal and get their ingredients for pizzaiola sauce.

She was so interesting that I stopped to talk with her. She'd been at the market most of her life. She was typical of the characters who you meet in an Italian market: full of humor, energy and hustle. I was completely charmed! And as I walked away from her stall with the ingredients for my pizzaiola sauce, I took some good-natured ribbing from the other vendors. Pizzaiola is a classic and really versatile Neapolitan tomato sauce, and it's another example of a recipe that every family has made their own way for generations. You can cook meat or fish right in the sauce. Or for an amazing snack, cut up some fresh mozzarella or provola and ladle the hot sauce right over it. Just make sure you have enough bread for *scarpetta*.

Heat up the olive oil in a pot over medium heat. Add the garlic and cook for about a minute, until soft. Be careful: You do not want to burn the garlic, or even let it turn golden. Add a few chili flakes for heat if you want to. Add the cherry tomatoes and stir in a tablespoon (15 mL) of the passata. Cook until the tomatoes start to soften, then add the remaining passata and the tomato paste and stir to combine. Then add the oregano and salt, and let it simmer for 15 minutes. Serve, garnished with a fresh basil leaf or two.

MAKES 2 1/2 CUPS (750 ML)

PASTA AL FORNO

1 lb (500 g) penne pasta

1/4 cup (60 mL) extra-virgin olive oil

2 cloves garlic, chopped

1 large eggplant, cubed

10 large sundried tomatoes

1 cup (250 mL) pitted black olives

2 dried chili flakes (optional)

2 cups (500 mL) passata

Salt, QB

1 cup (250 mL) ricotta

1 cup (250 mL) shredded mozzarella

1 cup (250 mL) smoked scamorza, roughly chopped

Freshly grated Parmigiano-Reggiano, QB

This is the first of two of my favorite baked pasta dishes that I am passing on to you. *So, David,* you might ask, *why did you start this baked pasta section with pasta al forno and not with the star dish in this category—lasagna?* Let me say for the record that I love both. But for some reason, even though they are similar in style and equally delicious, lasagna became the superstar dish, an iconic fixture in Italian restaurants around the globe, and pasta al forno, which honestly takes half the time to make, stayed a secret known and loved by Italian families. I'm on a mission to give pasta al forno its due. So it goes first.

This dish is very forgiving. It's probably the only time I will tell you that even if you overcook your pasta, everything will be okay in the end.

Start making your sauce and pasta at the same time.

Put a large pot of water on to boil. When the water boils, salt it and drop in the pasta. Give it a gentle stir.

Heat the olive oil in a large saucepan over medium-high heat. When the oil shimmers, add the garlic and cook just until it starts to brown. Now add the eggplant, sundried tomatoes, olives and chili flakes. Let it cook, stirring occasionally so that the eggplant doesn't stick, until the eggplant gets soft and golden. You may need to add a little more olive oil, but use a very light hand: Eggplant is like a sponge and will soak up the oil.

When the eggplant is golden, add the passata and some salt. Let it simmer for 5 or 10 minutes.

Preheat the oven to 400°F (200°C).

When the pasta is al dente, drain it and put it back in the pot. Then add the sauce to the pasta, along with the ricotta, mozzarella and scamorza, and give it a really good stir.

Pour everything into a lasagna pan. Sprinkle evenly with Parmigiano. Bake for about half an hour or until the sauce is bubbling and the top is slightly crisp around the edges. Take it out of the oven and let it rest for half an hour before serving.

SERVES 6

LASAGNA

1 batch Fresh Pasta Dough (page 13) or 1 lb (500 g) dried lasagna pasta sheets

1 batch Bolognese Sauce (page 23)

1 batch Salsa Besciamella (page 27)

14 oz (400 g) freshly grated mozzarella

Freshly grated Parmigiano-Reggiano, QB

Let's face it, everyone loves lasagna. It's just a fact.

It is labor-intensive—probably one of the most labor-intensive recipes in this book—but it's not hard. You can make lasagna with dried or fresh pasta. When I have time I like to make my own pasta, because it has a more delicate texture. But using dried pasta is absolutely fine.

Making lasagna is a great way to spend family time together on a Sunday. Everyone can help make the pasta, and the kids can help with the assembly by ladling in the tomato sauce.

If you're using fresh lasagna sheets: Put a large pot of water on to boil. When the water boils, generously salt it. Working in batches so you don't overcrowd the pot, cook the pasta for about a minute, just until it is tender but still firm. Scoop the pasta out of the pot and transfer it to a bowl of cold water. Let the pasta sit for a minute or two, just until it is cool enough to handle. Then lay it out on a clean kitchen towel while you continue to cook the rest of the pasta sheets. Don't stack them on top of each other to drain. Layer over another kitchen towel, if you need to.

If you're using dried lasagna sheets: You can put them directly into the baking dish without boiling them first. Just make sure your ragù is "saucy" or add 1 cup (250 mL) of passata to the ragù to loosen it. The extra liquid will cook the sheets as the lasagna bakes.

To assemble the lasagna: Preheat the oven to 375°F (190°C).

Cover the bottom of a lasagna pan with a layer of Bolognese Sauce. Next, put a layer of pasta sheets on top of the sauce, so they fully cover the pan. Top that with another generous layer of Bolognese Sauce. Now add a light layer of the Salsa Besciamella. Sprinkle evenly with some mozzarella, then some Parmigiano over that. In goes another layer of pasta and ragù, and you repeat the pattern for three or four layers. The final layer should be ragù with a good sprinkle of Parmigiano.

Bake for about 40 minutes, until the top is golden and the lasagna is cooked through. Take it out of the oven and let it rest for 20 minutes before serving. It tastes best when it's had a chance to cool down a bit.

SERVES 8

BRACIOLE

1 1/2 lb (750 g) flank steak, cut into 8 slices

Salt, QB

Freshly ground black pepper, QB

1 bunch fresh flat-leaf parsley, finely chopped

Handful of pine nuts

Handful of raisins

Handful of freshly grated pecorino

8 slices Parmigiano-Reggiano

1/4 cup (60 mL) extra-virgin olive oil

3 cloves garlic, smashed

1 cup (250 mL) red wine

4 cups (1 L) passata

In every American movie about Italian families, inevitably someone will either go home to eat Mamma's, or talk about eating his Mamma's, braciole. These scenes always make me laugh because they hit home! Braciole (pronounced *brazh-OL*) is the essence of Neapolitan comfort food.

When I was in Naples recently, my friend Luigi and his mom invited me for lunch, and she served us her version of braciole. Tasting it you would have thought she spent all morning fussing over it, but the truth is she did up the beef rolls in the morning and put them on the stove to simmer in tomato sauce for about 4 hours until we all met up for lunch. The lesson: Sometimes your stove is the best sous chef.

Her version of braciole is very similar to the way my family makes it—with lots of chopped parsley, raisins and pine nuts. But I liked her addition of thick slices of Parmigiano. So simple, and yet I think it's the best version I've ever had.

To prepare the beef rolls: First you need to flatten your flank steak. You can ask your butcher to do this for you, or you can do it yourself by putting the slices between two sheets of plastic wrap and pounding them with a meat mallet until they're about 1/4 inch (0.5 cm) thick.

Lay out the flattened slices of meat, and sprinkle with the salt, pepper, parsley, pine nuts, raisins and pecorino. Top each with a slice of Parmigiano. Roll them up and secure with either butcher's twine or a toothpick. Set aside.

For the sauce: Heat the olive oil in a pot over medium heat. When the oil shimmers, add the beef rolls and sear them until they're brown on all sides. Add the garlic and cook for 30 to 40 seconds. Add the red wine, stirring to pick up any brown bits on the bottom of the pan, and cook until the liquid is reduced by half. Now add the passata and some salt. Bring it to a light boil, and then reduce the heat, cover the pan with a lid and simmer for about 4 hours.

When it's done, remove the braciole from the sauce and discard the garlic. Cook up some pasta, use the ragù for the sauce and serve the braciole for your *secondo*.

SERVES 4 TO 6

MEATBALLS WITH TOMATO SAUCE

Meatballs

1 lb (500 g) extra-lean ground beef

1 lb (500 g) ground pork

1/2 cup (125 mL) ricotta

1 egg

1 cup (250 mL) freshly grated Parmigiano-Reggiano

1/2 bunch fresh flat-leaf parsley, chopped

Salt, QB

Freshly ground black pepper, QB

Tomato Sauce

1/4 cup (60 mL) extra-virgin olive oil

1 small onion, finely chopped

1 cup (250 mL) red wine

6 cups (1.5 L) passata

Salt, QB

Freshly ground black pepper, QB

It seems that everyone has their own version of meatballs. In my family, both my mom's side and my dad's side have different approaches. But when it comes to meatballs, there's never a bad one as far as I'm concerned.

This recipe actually gives you multiple serving options: You can serve the meatballs with the sauce over pasta. You can separate the meatballs from the sauce and use the sauce for your pasta and the meatballs for your *secondo*. These meatballs also make a great sandwich.

In a mixing bowl, combine the ground beef and pork, ricotta, egg, Parmigiano, parsley and salt and pepper. Mix well to combine all of the ingredients. Using your hands, scoop up the mixture and shape into balls about the size of a golf ball.

Heat the olive oil in a large saucepan over medium heat. When the oil shimmers, add the onion and cook until translucent. Then add the meatballs and the wine, and cook until the wine reduces by half. Add the passata and salt, and bring the mixture to a slight boil. Reduce the heat to medium-low and let it cook, uncovered, for about 90 minutes.

Turn off the heat and let it rest with a lid on for about an hour before serving.

SERVES 6 TO 8

POLLO AL MATTONE

1 whole chicken (4 lb/2 kg),
rinsed and patted dry

Juice of 1/2 lemon

1/4 cup (60 mL) extra-virgin olive
oil, divided

1 tbsp (15 mL) chopped fresh
rosemary

3 cloves garlic, crushed

Dried chili flakes, QB (optional)

Salt, QB

Freshly ground black pepper, QB

Al Mattone is not the name of my godfather! It's an Italian term that means "with a brick," and that's how you cook this chicken. This recipe calls for a whole chicken that is butterflied or spatchcocked and weighted down. You can use a brick wrapped in foil or a cast iron pan. The weight holds the chicken flat so that the skin gets nicely and uniformly crispy, and the rest of the bird stays moist and juicy.

If you do use an actual brick for this, make sure to use a brand-new brick, one that hasn't been used for anything else, and wrap it well in foil. There should be absolutely no direct contact between the meat and the surface of the brick.

Get your butcher to butterfly your chicken for you. Or you can do it yourself using kitchen scissors: Cut down each side of the backbone and remove it. Then using the palms of your hands, press down on the chicken so it's lying flat. Put the chicken in a plastic bag.

In a bowl, stir together the lemon juice, 2 tablespoons (30 mL) of olive oil, the rosemary and the garlic and, if you like, chili flakes. Pour it over the chicken in the bag, turning the chicken to coat well. Let the chicken rest in the fridge for at least 2 hours or, preferably, overnight.

Preheat your oven to 400°F (200°C).

Remove the chicken from the bag and season all over with salt and pepper.

Heat a grill pan until it's very hot. Add the remaining 2 tablespoons (30 mL) of olive oil to the pan, and put the chicken in skin-side down. Put a foil-wrapped brick or heavy cast iron pan on top of the chicken, and let it cook for 5 to 7 minutes, until the skin is golden.

Transfer the pan to the oven—you can remove the weight to make this easier, but make sure you put it back on once the pan is in the oven. Cook for 30 minutes. Remove the pan from the oven and take off the brick or pan. Flip the chicken over, and slide the pan back in the oven and cook for another 10 minutes or until the juices run clear. Take it out of the oven and let it rest for 10 minutes before serving.

SERVES 4

PESCE ALLA PUTTANESCA

1/4 cup (60 mL) extra-virgin olive oil

1 clove garlic, finely sliced

Dried chili flakes, QB

2 tsp (10 mL) anchovy paste

16 black olives, pitted

2 tbsp (30 mL) capers, drained

1 pint (25 to 30) cherry tomatoes

4 *branzino* or sea bass fillets (4 to 6 oz/125 to 175 g each)

Finely chopped fresh flat-leaf parsley, QB

1 glass dry white wine

Salt, QB

This takes elements of classic puttanesca pasta sauce—olives, capers and anchovies—and turns them into a flavorful poaching sauce for fish. It takes minutes to make, and works really well with any white fish.

Heat the olive oil in a frying pan over medium heat. Add the garlic, chili flakes, anchovy paste, olives and capers, and cook until the anchovy paste dissolves. Then add the tomatoes and cook until they soften and start to release their juices. Add the fish fillets, parsley, white wine and some salt. Cover the pan and let it cook for about 10 minutes, until the fish flakes easily.

SERVES 4

I MIEI DOLCETTI

BULL'S-EYE COOKIES

1 cup (250 mL) unsalted butter

2/3 cup (150 mL) granulated sugar

2 large eggs

1 tsp (5 mL) pure vanilla extract

2 cups (500 mL) Tipo 00 flour

1/4 tsp (1 mL) salt

1 tsp (5 mL) freshly grated lemon zest (optional)

1/2 cup (125 mL) good-quality raspberry jam

Icing sugar, for sprinkling

These white-and-red cookies resemble a bull's-eye target, hence the name. You'll find these at a lot of bars in Italy, filled with jam or sometimes Nutella. They look complicated but are honestly easy to make. I love them as a midday treat with my espresso.

With an electric mixer, or a stand mixer fitted with a paddle attachment, beat together the butter and sugar until fluffy and creamy. Then add the eggs and beat until incorporated. Mix in the vanilla.

In a separate bowl, combine the flour, salt and, if you want, lemon zest. Then add it to the wet ingredients. Mix everything together until well combined. You will end up with a nice smooth dough. Turn it out of the bowl onto a lightly floured work surface and knead it for a minute or so. Shape it into a ball and cover tightly with plastic wrap. Put it in the fridge for half an hour.

Preheat your oven to 350°F (180°C).

Take the chilled dough out of the fridge and unwrap it. Lightly dust your work surface with flour. Divide the dough into two equal portions. Roll each portion out to a sheet about 1/4 inch (0.5 cm) thick.

Using a 4-inch (10 cm) cookie cutter, cut out as many cookies as you can from one sheet and transfer them to a baking sheet lined with parchment paper. You should have 20 to 22 rounds.

Cut out the same number of cookies from the second sheet of dough and transfer them to a separate baking sheet lined with parchment paper. Then take a smaller cookie cutter (a 3-inch/7.5 cm one works well) and cut a hole in the middle of each in this second group. Reserve the "holes" and bake them separately for a small treat.

Bake for 12 to 15 minutes, until lightly golden. Keep your eye on them. Some ovens are hotter than others and yours may cook faster. You may need to rotate the pans or take them out sooner. Remove the pans from the oven and place them on wire racks to cool completely.

When the cookies are cool, spread jam on one side of the cookies without the hole, making sure you have a bit more jam in the center. Sprinkle the second group of cookies—the ones with the hole—with icing sugar until they're nicely covered. Holding the powdered cookies by the edges, place each one on top of a jam cookie to form a sandwich, being careful not to press down too firmly. Store them in an airtight container for up to a week or freeze them for about 6 months.

MAKES 20 TO 22 COOKIES

NUTELLA BOMBOLONI

A *bomboloni* is a traditional Italian doughnut that can be filled with an assortment of sweet things: cream, jam, custard or, my favorite, Nutella.

I love making *bomboloni* for the kids—but the truth is that although I say I'm making it for them, when it comes to the last one, we all do rock, paper, scissors to see who gets it, and no one is a good loser.

This is a fantastic thing to do on a lazy Sunday. They're not hard to make, but you need time because the dough has to proof. The instructions here call for a stand mixer, but you can also knead the dough by hand.

---

1 cup (250 mL) milk, room temperature, divided

1/2 oz (15 g) fresh yeast or 1/4 oz (7 g) active dry yeast

1 large egg + 2 large egg yolks

2 cups (500 mL) all-purpose flour, plus more as needed

1/2 cup (125 mL) granulated sugar, plus more for coating

2 tsp (10 mL) salt

Zest of 1 lemon

1/4 cup (60 mL) butter, room temperature

Vegetable oil, for frying

1 jar (14 oz/400 g) Nutella

Heat 1/3 cup (75 mL) of milk until just lukewarm. Add the yeast, and stir it with your finger until it dissolves. Set aside.

In a bowl, whisk together the egg, egg yolks and the remaining 2/3 cup (150 mL) milk.

In the bowl of a stand mixer fitted with the dough hook, combine the flour, sugar, salt and lemon zest. Mix it together. While mixing, gradually add the egg and milk mixture. Then add the yeast mixture, and continue to mix until combined. Add the butter, a little at a time, and mix until it's all incorporated. The dough should be very soft but not sticky. If the dough is sticking to the bowl, sprinkle in a little flour and mix, adding just enough flour so the dough comes away from the sides of the bowl.

Turn the dough out onto a lightly floured work surface. Using your hands, knead it for a minute, until it comes together in a nice ball. Place the ball in a bowl and cover the bowl with plastic wrap. Let it sit until it the dough doubles in size, which will take about 3 hours. So take a break, walk the dog or have a nap.

Once your dough has risen, turn it out onto a lightly floured work surface. With a rolling pin, roll the dough out until it's about 3/4 inch (2 cm) thick.

Using a round pastry cutter the size of a cup, cut the dough into disks. Reroll any scraps and repeat until you have used up all of the dough.

Transfer each round to a sheet pan lined with parchment paper. Cover the whole thing with plastic wrap. Now let the dough sit for another hour and a half. I'd suggest a second nap.

Take out two plates or baking sheets. Line one with a few pieces of paper towel and pour the sugar for coating on the other. Set aside.

Fill a large, heavy-bottomed saucepan halfway with vegetable oil and place over high heat. You need to get the oil really hot. You can use a deep-fry thermometer to test the oil if you like, but I don't. I just

drop in a pinch of the dough; if it fries immediately, it's good to go. If you use a thermometer, heat the oil to 350°F (180°C).

Working in small batches, carefully drop the rounds into the hot oil and fry until the bottom is golden. Flip them over and fry the other side until golden. The whole thing should take 3 to 5 minutes. When the *bomboloni* are done, use a slotted spoon to transfer them to the paper towels to absorb any excess oil. While they're still hot, roll them in the sugar until covered. Put them on wire racks or a plate to cool slightly. Repeat with the remaining rounds.

Fill a pastry bag fitted with a 1/2 inch (1 cm) pastry tip with the Nutella. Poke the tip three-quarters of the way into the doughnut and squeeze the bag, pulling the tip back slowly as you go so that you add as much filling as possible. Repeat with remaining *bomboloni*.

Serve warm or at room temperature. They're delicious.

MAKES 12 TO 14 DOUGHNUTS

SWEET CARROZZA

I love the combination of mascarpone and Nutella. The mascarpone tones down the sweetness of the Nutella and gives it an even more silky, luxurious texture. I often combine the two on *pizza bianca* for a delicious dessert pizza. Sweet carrozza is another way to combine the two. It's a spin on the classic Neapolitan grilled cheese sandwich, *mozzarella in carrozza*. It's easy to make, and you can get the kids involved, spreading the cheese and the Nutella on the bread.

12 slices white sandwich bread

Nutella, QB

Mascarpone, QB

2 bananas, sliced into rounds

1 tbsp (15 mL) extra-virgin olive oil

4 large eggs

Icing sugar, for dusting

For this recipe, I recommend using a non-stick pan if you have one. For each sandwich, cover one slice of bread with Nutella and the other with mascarpone. It's all *quanto basta,* so you can take liberties on how decadent you want to make these. Put a few slices of banana on one side and close it up as you would any sandwich.

Heat the olive oil in a frying pan over medium heat.

Beat the eggs in a shallow bowl. Dip each sandwich in the eggs, completely coating both sides. Working in batches, transfer the coated sandwiches to the frying pan, and fry on both sides until golden.

To serve, cut each sandwich in half and dust with icing sugar.

MAKES 6 SANDWICHES

CIAMBELLE

5 cups (1.25 L) all-purpose flour

1 cup (250 mL) granulated sugar, plus more for dredging (optional)

1 cup (250 mL) extra-virgin olive oil

1 cup (250 mL) dry white wine

2 tbsp (30 mL) aniseeds

Ciambelle is a biscotti, a semi-hard cookie that is great for dipping in milk, coffee, wine or, as I like to do, Vin Santo. I got this recipe in Sicily. When I first saw it, I was surprised at the quantities—a cup of olive oil?! But it works beautifully.

Ciambelle are easy to make. Because the sugar, olive oil and wine are all in equal proportions, it's easy to adjust the recipe to make fewer or more. Once you get the dough together, you can get your kids to roll out the ciambelle.

Preheat your oven to 400°F (200°C). Line a baking sheet with parchment paper.

You can mix this together in a bowl, but it's more fun to pour it on a clean counter and go full *nonna*. So, if you're going to do that, pour the flour on the counter (or in your bowl) and make a well in the center. Then pour everything else into the well. Get your hands in there and start combining everything together until you end up with a dough that is firm but not too sticky, like a strong bread dough. You might need a little more or less flour than I've recommended, so work by eye.

Pinch off a small amount of dough and roll it into a 1/2-inch (2.5 cm) thick log. Cut the log into 4-inch (10 cm) lengths. Bring the ends of each piece together to make a doughnut shape, then pinch the ends to close them. Keep going until you've used up all of the dough. If you want, you can dredge the cookies in sugar to add a sweet crunch.

Place the ciambelle on the baking sheet, spacing them about 2 inches (5 cm) apart. Bake for about 10 minutes or until golden brown. Transfer the cookies to wire racks to cool. Store in an airtight container for up to a week or freeze them for even longer.

MAKES ABOUT 24 COOKIES

CHOCOLATE ESPRESSO COOKIES

1/4 cup (60 mL) butter

2/3 cup (150 mL) packed brown sugar

1 large egg

4 oz (125 g) semisweet chocolate, melted and cooled

1/2 cup (125 mL) all-purpose flour

1/4 cup (60 mL) unsweetened cocoa powder

4 tsp (20 mL) instant espresso coffee granules

1 tsp (5 mL) baking powder

Pinch of salt

1 tbsp (15 mL) milk

Icing sugar, for dredging

These are the ultimate adult cookies. Not too sweet, and the backdrop of espresso deepens the cocoa taste. They are fabulous with coffee. We often make these at Christmastime.

In the bowl of your stand mixer, use the paddle attachment to cream together the butter and brown sugar until light and fluffy. Then beat in the egg until incorporated. Fold in the cooled chocolate.

In a separate bowl, sift together the flour, cocoa powder, instant espresso, baking powder and salt. With the mixer on low speed, add the dry ingredients to the wet ingredients (the dough will be a little sticky), and then add the milk and mix until combined. Turn the dough out onto your work surface. Using your hands or a rolling pin, flatten the dough into a disk. Wrap it tightly in plastic wrap and put it in the freezer until the dough is firm, about 45 minutes.

Preheat your oven to 350°F (180°C). Line two baking sheets with parchment paper. Pour some icing sugar onto a plate.

Shape the dough into 1-inch (2.5 cm) balls (approx.). Roll each ball in the icing sugar several times—you want them to be completely covered in sugar so that no dough shows through—and put it on a baking sheet, spacing each about 2 inches (5 cm) apart. Don't crowd them.

Bake for 12 to 15 minutes, until the cookies have spread and cracked. The dark chocolate will show through the white sugar coating, which gives them a nice finish.

Transfer the cookies to wire racks to cool. Store in an airtight container for up to a week or freeze them for even longer.

MAKES ABOUT 24 COOKIES

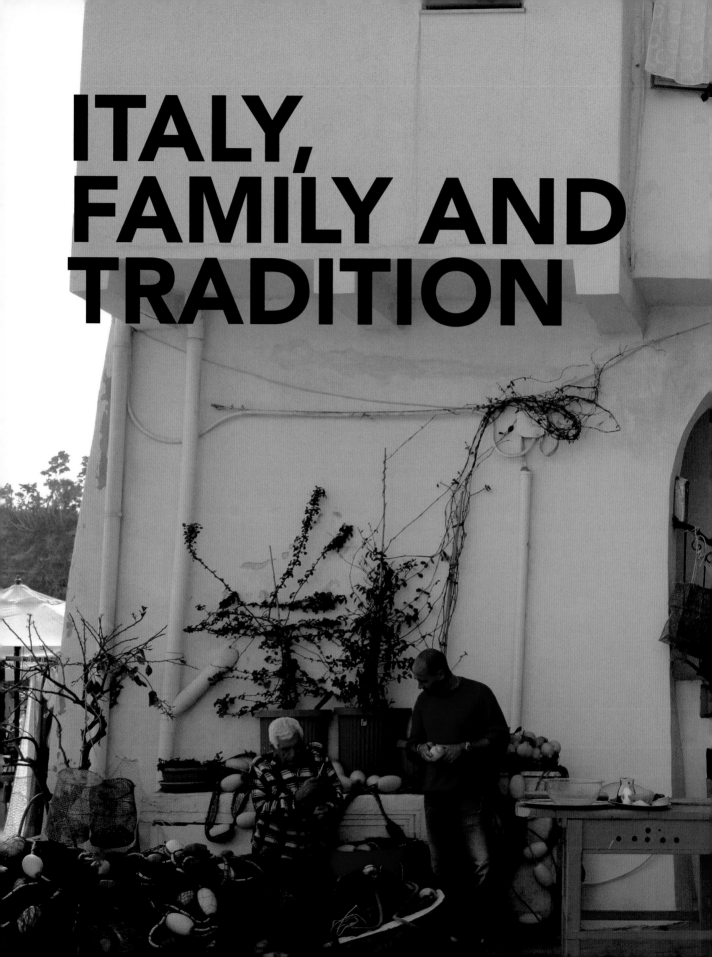

ITALY, FAMILY AND TRADITION

You cannot overstate the importance of tradition in Italy—for better and for worse. It's what makes Italy such an incredible place, and also what makes it so deliciously dysfunctional. The importance of heritage is especially evident when it comes to food.

You grow up in a family where your parents and grandparents are always cooking, and you all eat together. From your earliest days you learn to do things the way your family does and always has done.

If your family is in the business of producing one of Italy's iconic products, such as wine, olive oil, Aceto Balsamico di Modena or Parmigiano-Reggiano, chances are the business has been in the family for generations. You grow up being groomed to be the next one to take it over.

For some people, the idea of staying in one place to carry forward the family legacy could be stifling. But for many, many people in Italy, the tie to their traditions is like oxygen. It gives them a profession

and the motivation to strive for excellence. It also gives them a sense of having a place in the world that matters. It may only matter to their local community, but that is a source of pride and joy.

And when you step into the family business, you are aware that you are the gatekeeper of a specific tradition, taking it from the past to the future. And since what you're producing is food, you're making something that you share. You can see the reactions when people taste your food and take it home to enjoy with their family. Food is a medium that brings people together, and in Italy this is a truth that runs deep within the fabric of the people.

The pride in being a chef, a butcher, a grower or a parent cooking for a child is evident. In this next part of the book I want to introduce you to some people who have taken up the family mantle with pride. They've deepened my appreciation for artisanal products and influenced the way I cook.

CARLOTTA THE WINEMAKER

arlotta Pometti, who is still in her twenties, is one of the youngest winemakers in Italy. Her family has owned land in Tuscany near the town of Trequanda, just outside of Siena, since the 1600s. They produce wine, grappa, extra-virgin olive oil and pecorino cheese. Carlotta oversees the family's businesses, including the agriturismos: Fattoria La Selva and Pometti, which are on the grounds of their working farm.

When you're living and working on the land that your family has owned for more than 400 years, that's really something special: If you think about it, some of what you harvest was planted by the hands of your ancestors. I think that's kind of cool.

From the first moment I met Carlotta, she struck me as someone who was wise beyond her years. I could see that a sense of pride and responsibility to keep what her family has built over centuries was in her blood. And she's an amazing cook. She learned by cooking with her Nonna Marisa. Carlotta really loves making those recipes and keeping them alive. She often prepares them with her guests. Having said all of that, she's also a woman in her late twenties. She's a lot of fun.

When I visit Carlotta, there's no question that we're going to end up in the kitchen cooking together. We both have the same philosophy about food and a similar approach to making it.

I remember one year I was there in early July. There were some American guests, so we decided to make a Fourth of July feast for them—Tuscan-style. We cooked together, and it was effortless, casual and just like family.

SPINACH RAVIOLI

2 bunches of fresh spinach or 1 bag (9 to 10 oz/280 to 300 g) frozen spinach

1 lb (500 g) ricotta (preferably sheep's milk)

Salt, QB

Freshly ground black pepper, QB

1 large egg

1/2 cup (125 mL) freshly grated Parmigiano-Reggiano

1 batch Fresh Pasta Dough (page 13)

One of the first things Carlotta and I bonded over was our mutual love of spinach ravioli. Probably the only person who likes it more is my wife, Nina. Wherever we eat them, no matter where we are, Nina says, "This reminds me of my Nonna Maria." It's total comfort food.

You don't have to have an Italian Nonna to love ravioli, or to make them. Making them is much easier than you might expect, and the payoff is that the dough is so much silkier.

The trick with this ravioli is actually making sure that the spinach is as dry as possible before you begin. If the spinach is too moist, the ravioli will fall apart before you even get them in the pot.

I'll give you starting quantities, but my general rule of thumb is one part cooked spinach to one part ricotta. The Parmigiano adds flavor, but it also acts as a binder and further absorbs any moisture in the filling.

If you are using fresh spinach: Clean it well. In a dry pan over medium-high heat, combine a couple of tablespoons (30 mL) of water and the spinach and cook until the spinach wilts. Remove it from the heat and let it cool. When it's cool enough to handle, squeeze it over the sink to remove as much water as you can. Then finely chop the spinach and put it in a mixing bowl.

If you are using frozen spinach: Let it thaw. Squeeze out any excess water over the sink, then finely chop it and put it in a mixing bowl.

To the bowl of spinach, add the ricotta with some salt and pepper, and the egg and Parmigiano, and mix well.

To make the ravioli: Cut off a piece of the fresh pasta dough, about the size of a tennis ball. Flatten it with the palms of your hand so it is thin enough to start running it through your pasta machine. (See Using a Pasta Machine, page 16.) You should end up with a nice long, thin sheet of pasta. Put it on a baking sheet and cover with a damp kitchen towel. Repeat until all the dough is used up.

Dust your work surface with a bit of flour, so the pasta doesn't stick, and lay one of the sheets down. Now the fun part.

recipe continues . . .

You're going to put your mounds of filling in a row across the sheet of pasta. Place the sheet of pasta lengthwise on the counter. Starting on the left side, put a tablespoon (15 mL) of the ricotta-spinach filling about 1 inch (2.5 cm) from the left edge and 1 inch (2.5 cm) or so from the bottom edge. Repeat across the length of the sheet. Fold the top of the pasta sheet over the ricotta mounds so that it meets the other edge. Using the side of your hand, press the edge to seal it. Then press down between each mound of filling to make the individual ravioli pockets. This should also get rid of any trapped air.

To cut the ravioli: Using a pasta cutter wheel, cut along the entire unfinished edge of the pasta, just a little under the filling. Then cut between each ravioli. If you don't have a pasta cutter wheel, you can use a small, sharp knife. Just gently press along the edges of the ravioli with your fingers to make sure they're sealed.

If each ravioli is different in size and shape, bravo! That's the point. They're homemade, *nonna*-style.

At this point you can freeze them if you want. Arrange them in a single layer on a baking sheet and put them in the freezer. Once they're frozen, transfer them to airtight containers or freezer bags. They'll keep for about 3 or 4 months, and you can cook them right from frozen.

To cook the ravioli: Fill a pot with water and add the salt and a tablespoon (15 mL) of olive oil to prevent them from sticking. This isn't like dry pasta where you can stir it. The ravioli are delicate, so don't overcrowd the pot. Once your water is boiling, drop in a few at a time. When they rise to the top, after about 3 minutes, use a slotted spoon to transfer them to a serving bowl.

You can serve the ravioli with your favorite sauce, but they're so flavorful that I often just drizzle them with some good olive oil and finish with some freshly grated Parmigiano.

SERVES 6

TUSCAN PICI

Pici (pronounced "peachy") is a traditional Tuscan long pasta. It's probably the easiest pasta to make. It doesn't require any machines or special equipment. The dough is rolled with the palm of your hand into long strands like shoelaces, which are then cut up into smaller lengths and cooked. Trust me, this will make you feel like you're back in kindergarten playing with Plasticine.

Carlotta introduced me to a woman she calls Zia Isa. Isa is not Carlotta's blood relative but a lifelong family friend and a local expert at making this traditional pasta. She taught me to make this, and now I'm passing it on to you.

Now, just a note: I've made this with the Fresh Pasta Dough recipe on page 13 and I've made it Zia Isa's way. Both work, so it's up to you. It's also an interesting fact about Italian cooking: Recipes differ from town to town, family to family. Drive a hundred miles from where you are and you'll likely find a slight variation, even in a traditional dish.

2 cups (500 mL) semolina flour

2 cups (500 mL) all-purpose flour

1 large egg

1 to 1 1/2 cups (250 to 375 mL) lukewarm water

To make the pasta dough: Pour both flours onto a work surface and mix together. Make a well in the middle. Put the egg into the well and, using your fork, start to whisk, pulling the flour into the egg as you go. When the egg is incorporated, add the water, a bit at a time, continuing to stir until you have used up all the water. Now put your fork aside and use your hands to knead the dough, using the palm of your hand to first push the dough away from you, and then to roll it back. Keep going until the dough has formed a smooth and shiny ball that has a nice elasticity to it. You can check by pressing your finger lightly into the surface of the dough. If the dough springs back, you're done! This takes 5 or 6 minutes. When you're there, cover the dough with plastic wrap and set it aside to rest for half an hour.

To shape the pici: Pull off a golf ball–size chunk of dough. Lightly dust your work surface with flour and, using the palm of your hand, roll the dough into a long noodle about 1/2 inch (1 cm) thick. Cut that into 4- or 5-inch (10 or 12.5 cm) lengths. Repeat with the remaining dough.

At this point you can freeze the pici if you want. Arrange them in a single layer on a baking sheet and put them in the freezer. Once they're frozen, transfer them to airtight containers or freezer bags. They'll keep for about 3 or 4 months, and you can cook them right from frozen.

To cook the pici: Bring a pot of water to a boil. When the water boils, salt it and drop in the pici. Give them a quick stir. They will take only 2 to 3 minutes to cook. When they rise to the surface, transfer them to a serving plate using a slotted spoon. They're ready to eat. They'll work with any sauce, including Pici Aglio e Olio con Crostini (page 136) and My Palio Pasta (page 208).

SERVES 6

PICI AGLIO E OLIO CON CROSTINI

1 cup (250 mL) extra-virgin olive oil, divided

Day-old Tuscan bread, or country-style bread, cut into crouton-size pieces, QB

1 tbsp (15 mL) anchovy paste

Freshly cracked black pepper, QB

1 lb (500 g) fresh pici pasta, spaghetti or other long pasta

1/2 cup (125 mL) freshly grated pecorino

When I'm in Tuscany, where the olive oil is always fresh and abundant, I find myself looking for ways to cook with it. And at Carlotta's, where they have their own olive oil, which is some of the best around, a dish like this takes advantage of it.

Heat 1/2 cup (125 mL) of the olive oil in a frying pan over medium-high heat. When the oil shimmers, add the bread cubes in small batches and cook until golden. As they finish cooking, transfer them to a plate lined with paper towels to absorb any excess oil.

Put a pot of water on to boil to cook your pasta. The pici will cook very quickly, so while you're waiting for the water to boil, make your sauce.

In a frying pan over low heat, heat up the remaining 1/2 cup (125 mL) olive oil. Add the anchovy paste and pepper, and stir until the anchovy paste dissolves.

When the water boils, salt it and drop in the pasta. Give it a gentle stir. The pici will rise to the surface when they're done.

Drain the cooked pasta, reserving about 1/3 cup (75 mL) of the pasta cooking water, and then add them to the frying pan, along with the toasted croutons, and toss together. Remove the pan from the heat and add the pecorino, giving it a few more tosses to combine.

Serve immediately.

SERVES 4

PORK IN CROSTA

2 tbsp (30 mL) extra-virgin olive oil, plus more for drizzling

2 lb (1 kg) pork or beef tenderloin

Salt, QB

Freshly ground black pepper, QB.

1 bunch fresh sage, leaves only, finely chopped

1 bunch fresh rosemary, needles only, finely chopped

1 loaf crusty Tuscan-style bread (long enough to cover the entire piece of meat)

8 to 10 long, thin slices of prosciutto or pancetta, thinly sliced

Sometimes you come across a recipe that is so incredibly easy and so incredibly delicious that it's like a gift.

I had this on my first visit to Carlotta's agriturismo and loved it. The following year when I went back I asked if I could have it again, so they gave me the ingredients, the broad strokes of the recipe and told me to go for it! In essence, it takes ordinary Tuscan ingredients—sage, rosemary, olive oil, Tuscan bread—and with no fancy techniques makes something special. The bread gets crunchy and the meat stays moist and is flavored by the herbs. It works equally well with pork or beef tenderloin. In fact, you can think of it as a simple Tuscan farmer's pork or beef Wellington.

My family loves it, and it's become part of our repertoire.

Preheat your oven to 400°F (200°C).

Heat 2 tbsp (30 mL) of the olive oil in a frying pan over high heat. When it shimmers, sear the meat on all sides. Transfer the seared meat to a plate and season with salt and pepper.

In a small bowl, combine the sage and rosemary. Massage them into the meat and set aside.

Cut the loaf of bread in half lengthwise, leaving it attached on one side. Open it like a book and pull out some of the *mollica* (soft bread) from the middle (you can either eat it or discard it).

Put the meat on the bottom half of the loaf. If you want, you can top it with any of the herb mixture that's left. Close the bread so that it covers the meat. I like to drizzle more olive oil over the bread at this point, but I'll leave that up to you.

Lay the prosciutto or pancetta widthwise across the bread, covering the top of the loaf. To hold it all together, wrap it in kitchen twine. Put the *in crosta* on a baking sheet or oven-proof dish.

Roast for about 40 minutes, until the pork reaches an internal temperature of 160°F (71°C). Remove it from the oven and let it rest for 10 minutes so the juices redistribute.

Slice and serve.

SERVES 4 TO 6

CANTUCCI

1 cup (250 mL) granulated sugar

1/2 cup (125 mL) unsalted butter, melted

1 shot glass (1 1/2 oz/ 45 mL) Vin Santo or sweet port wine

3 large eggs

1 tbsp (15 mL) freshly grated orange zest

2 3/4 cups (675 mL) all-purpose flour

1 1/2 tsp (7 mL) baking powder

1/4 tsp (1 mL) salt

1 cup (250 mL) whole raw almonds, toasted and coarsely chopped

Countless family meals have been finished with these humble *biscotti*.

Unlike desserts that are eaten quickly and seem to signal the end of the meal, cantucci are an invitation to linger. For me the appearance of a plate of cantucci always signals a longer stay at the table. You can eat them as is, but these dried cookies beg to be dipped into espresso or Vin Santo.

At Carlotta's our dinners always seemed to end with us sitting around the table laughing, dipping our cookies and making small talk as the heat of the day gave way to cool evenings.

Mix together the sugar and butter. Add the eggs, Vin Santo or port, and orange zest and mix until combined. Add the flour, baking powder and salt and mix just until everything comes together. Add the almonds and mix just until they're evenly incorporated into the dough. Cover the dough with a kitchen towel and let rest for about half an hour.

Preheat your oven to 350°F (180°C). Line a baking sheet with parchment paper.

Divide the dough into two equal portions. Using your hands, shape the dough into two long baguette-shaped loaves and bake for 25 to 30 minutes, until the loaves are lightly golden on top.

Remove the pan from the oven and let the loaves cool until you can handle them. Using a serrated knife, carefully cut each loaf widthwise into 1/2 to 3/4 inch (1 to 2 cm) pieces.

Arrange the cookies, cut-side down, on the baking sheet and bake for another 15 to 20 minutes. You can eat these warm or let them cool completely and store in an airtight container. Because they're dried out, they'll last for a few weeks.

MAKES ABOUT 24 COOKIES

ACETO BALSAMICO DI MODENA

So I am walking around Modena, Italy, with a guy who can tell you what his great-great-great-great-great-etc. grandparents were doing in their day. I'll tell you: They were living in the same place that he does and making wine and balsamic vinegar.

Angelo Giacobazzi carries himself like a man who knows who he is and loves what he does. And who wouldn't when you are the latest in a long line of people producing a world-class condiment that at its very best is called "black gold"?

True balsamic vinegar has to be made in the Reggio Emilia and Modena area in Italy. That's its birthplace. There are references to its existence as a prized commodity as early as the eleventh century, but no one knows for sure just how far back families in the area were making it.

So when I said the words "balsamic vinegar" to Angelo he literally stopped in his tracks. *Ma Dai!*

"No. No. No," he said to me. "It is 'Aceto Balsamico *di Modena*.'"

Di Modena is too important a detail to leave off. And that's more than pride talking. It's like this: When you take up the family business, you're the new gatekeeper of that tradition. You are carrying that mantle forward. It's a huge responsibility and not something that Angelo, or any of the producers and vendors in Modena, take lightly. To make true Aceto Balsamico di Modena is a serious commitment that takes real dedication and the belief that you are doing something worthwhile.

Imagine starting something today that requires meticulous work when you know you're not going to see or taste it for three or twelve years—and that's for the stuff you use daily. Or for twenty-five years or even longer if you're making the thick, lush, pricey Aceto Balsamico Tradizionale, where just a drop is enough to make an atheist believe in heaven. When you taste it, you feel all of that passion and commitment that has gone into this exquisite-tasting product. Balsamic vinegar isn't a cooking ingredient per se—especially the good stuff. It's used as a finish to elevate a dish. A little drizzle is transformative, so taste is everything.

Balsamic vinegar is made from one of two kinds of grapes: Lambrusco or Trebbiano. The grapes are harvested and pressed. Then the stems, seeds, skin and juice—all of it—is poured into an open pot and simmered until it's reduced to one-third of its original volume. From there the concentrated liquid is poured and sealed into barrels and, over time, transferred into barrels of ever-decreasing sizes made of a variety of woods: oak, mulberry, chestnut, cherry and juniper. The vinegar picks up the flavor of each of the woods. As the liquid sits, evaporation takes place. The texture gets thicker, the flavor more concentrated and more complex. Throughout the process, it's checked and rechecked to make sure it has the right balance of flavor and acidity. The longer it sits, the more liquid evaporates. A really old *balsamico* can run you $100 to $200 for a very small bottle.

There are great stories about the production of Aceto Balsamico di Modena. Back in the day, the husbands and wives would bargain over who would get which part of the grape harvest. Traditionally the wives would want a share to make *balsamico,* and the husbands would be thinking about making wine. The negotiations would go on, I'm imagining, around the dinner table as they drank wine and drizzled some *balsamico* on some fabulous cheese.

The quality of a family's balsamic vinegar would be something to boast about. When a child was born, the family would set aside a barrel from their birth year to give to them when they got married. It's that important.

SALUMERIA GIUSTI

Officially, Salumeria Giusti in Modena was founded in 1605, but the owners say that Giovanni Giusti actually started producing and selling pork products in 1598. Either way, the Salumeria is the oldest deli in Europe and, quite possibly, the world.

Salumeria Giusti is still in the same location in which it started. It's a beautifully maintained little shop that sells the produce from the area—Prosciutto di Parma, Parmigiano-Reggiano, Grana Padano, fresh olive oil and, of course, a range of Aceto Balsamico di Modena. You can buy a relatively inexpensive bottle for daily use, or treat yourself to the Tradizionale.

Until 1980, the shop was owned by the descendants of Giovanni. At that point Giuseppe Giusti, who didn't have children to pass the business on to, sold it to perhaps the closest thing he had to a relative—Adriano Morandi, who had worked with the Giusti family since he was a child.

Now it's Adriano's children, Matteo and Cecilia, who have taken up the business. They run it as if it had been in their family all along.

ZUCCHINI FLAN

4 cups (1 L) vegetable stock

3 to 4 zucchini, cut into large chunks

1/2 cup (125 mL) freshly grated Parmigiano-Reggiano

1 cup (250 mL) whipping (35%) cream

4 large eggs

1 tsp (5 mL) salt

Extra-virgin olive oil, for greasing and drizzling

6 slices prosciutto

Aceto Balsamico di Modena, for drizzling

I had this flan when I was with Matteo and Cecilia at their hosteria. It's a simple family recipe that goes back generations. It has a silky, smooth, luxurious texture that is an excellent backdrop to the salty, crispy prosciutto and the sweet-acidic balsamic vinegar. I absolutely loved this, and they were kind enough to share their family recipe.

Preheat your oven to 350°F (180°C).

In a large pot, bring the vegetable stock to a boil. Add the zucchini and cook until the zucchini is soft, about 5 minutes. Drain and set aside to cool.

In a blender, combine the cooked zucchini, Parmigiano, cream, eggs and salt. Blend until smooth. Taste to see if it needs more salt or Parmigiano, and adjust the seasonings.

Brush individual 1/2-cup (125 mL) ramekins with olive oil. Fill each ramekin two-thirds full with the zucchini mixture. Place the ramekins in a large, deep pan. To the pan, add an inch (2.5 cm) of boiling water to create a water bath (*bain-marie*). Cover the pan with foil.

Place the pan in the oven and cook for 25 to 30 minutes, until they're set in the center. Remove the pan from the oven and let cool.

Once cool, remove the ramekins from the pan and put them in the fridge. Let sit for a few hours, until they solidify.

Before serving, preheat your oven to 400°F (200°C). Line a baking sheet with parchment paper.

Arrange the slices of prosciutto in a single layer on the baking sheet, making sure the edges aren't touching. Bake until crisp, about 5 minutes. Remove the pan from the oven and set aside to cool.

While the prosciutto is cooling, reduce the oven temperature to 300°F (150°C). Put the flans on a baking sheet and slide it into the oven for about 5 minutes or until heated through.

To unmold, gently run a knife around the inside of each ramekin and invert onto a serving plate.

Drizzle with olive oil and balsamic vinegar. Serve with a slice of crispy prosciutto on top.

MAKES 6 INDIVIDUAL FLANS

COTECHINO WITH LAMBRUSCO ZABAGLIONE

Cotechino is a traditional Northern Italian fresh sausage made with pork, pork rinds, lard and spices. In Italian tradition it's served with lentils on New Year's Day to bring good luck.

When I was visiting the Hosteria Giusti and saw *cotechino* on their menu, I had to have it. And as soon as I tasted it, I fell in love with the way they prepared it. It had a crispy coating and a soft, creamy interior. The Lambrusco Zabaglione took it to another level.

If you don't want to make the zabaglione, you can simply drizzle some extra-aged balsamic on the fried cotechino before serving.

This may seem like a complicated dish, but it's actually quite simple. It's old-style cooking that *nonne* make for their families.

Cotechino

1 lb (500 g) cotechino sausage

1 large egg

Plain dry bread crumbs, QB

1/3 cup (75 mL) extra-virgin olive oil

Aceto Balsamico di Modena, QB (optional)

Lambrusco Zabaglione

4 egg yolks

1/4 cup (60 mL) granulated sugar

1/3 glass Lambrusco wine (about 1/4 cup/60 mL)

Place the sausage in a saucepan, cover it with water and bring to a boil. Cook for about 30 minutes. Drain it, then let it cool. When the cotechino is cool enough to handle, cut it out of the casing and into 1-inch (2.5 cm) slices.

You need two bowls. In one, beat the egg. In the other, place the bread crumbs. Dip each slice of cooked cotechino first in the beaten egg and then in the bread crumbs, making sure each slice is completely coated.

Heat the olive oil in a frying pan over medium-high heat. When it shimmers, fry the breaded cotechino until golden on both sides. Using a slotted spoon, transfer the fried cotechino to a plate lined with paper towels to absorb any excess oil, and put it in a 200°F (100°C) oven to keep it warm while you prepare the zabaglione.

To make the zabaglione: Set up a double boiler: Pour water into a pot that is narrow enough that a metal mixing bowl can rest on the rim without falling in. You want to make sure that there's enough water in the pot to create steam to cook the ingredients, but you don't want the bowl to come into direct contact with the water. Bring the water to a boil and then reduce the heat to a good simmer.

Whisk together the eggs, sugar and Lambrusco in the metal mixing bowl. Place the bowl over the simmering water and start whisking like your life depends on it. You want to keep whisking so you don't end up with scrambled eggs. If the temperature seems too hot at any point, lift the bowl from the pot for a few seconds. After some whisking, you should end up with a zabaglione that is creamy and slightly foamy.

Once the zabaglione is ready, take the cotechino out of the oven and divide them among your serving plates. Ladle the creamy zabaglione over top and serve.

SERVES 4

FRESH TORTELLINI

1 batch (500 g) Fresh Pasta
Dough (page 13)

Filling

4 oz (125 g) pork tenderloin

2 oz (60 g) mortadella

2 oz (60 g) prosciutto

1 tsp (5 mL) ground nutmeg

1/4 tsp (2 mL) salt

2 oz (60 g) freshly grated
Parmigiano-Reggiano

1 egg

8 cups (2 L) chicken stock or
water

Sauce

3 tbsp (45 mL) butter

4 fresh sage leaves

1 tbsp (5 mL) all-purpose
flour

1/2 cup (125 mL) chicken
stock or water

Aceto Balsamico di Modena,
for drizzling

I was taught how to make fresh tortellini by master pasta maker Chef Maurizio Guidotti, who has a restaurant just outside of Modena. I have to admit that when I first started working with him, he was more than a bit intense and I was uncomfortable. And for a while I wondered if it was even worth being there. But I quickly realized that his intensity came from his passion and love for the tradition of making fresh pasta—specifically, tortellini. They're like little jewels to him. Maurizio was taught to make tortellini by his mother, who learned from her mother. It had been handed down that way for generations. Later on we had dinner together and I met his daughter, who told me that she had already learned the family's way of making various pastas and was committed to preserving those techniques.

To make the filling: Put the pork, mortadella and prosciutto in a food processor and pulse until fine and almost creamy. Scrape that into a mixing bowl and add the nutmeg, a pinch of salt, and the Parmigiano and egg. Use your hands to mix it all together. Let this rest for about 15 minutes.

To make the tortellini: Once the pasta dough has rested, pull off a good handful and flatten it between the palms of your hands. You can either roll it through a pasta machine (see Using a Pasta Machine, page 16) or you roll it out with a rolling pin. The goal is to end up with very thin sheets of pasta.

Lightly dust your work surface with some flour. Place the pasta sheet down and, using a pasta cutter wheel, cut it into 1-inch (2.5 cm) squares. If you want, you can use a ruler or the side of your rolling pin as a guide to help keep the lines straight.

Place about 1/2 tsp (2 mL) of the stuffing in the center of each square. Then fold the dough diagonally to make a little triangle. Now bear with me while I explain this next bit: You want to pull the two short sides of the triangle together and pinch them to make and seal the tortellini. Here's what I do to make it easier: I wrap each triangle around my index finger, which makes it easy to pinch the ends together.

At this point you can freeze them, if you like. Put the tortellini in a single layer on a baking sheet and slide it into the freezer. After about an hour or so, transfer the frozen tortellini to airtight containers or freezer bags. They will keep in the freezer for 3 to 4 months. You can cook them straight from frozen.

To cook the tortellini: In the Emilia-Romagna area they cook the tortellini in chicken stock, which adds extra flavor. You can, of course, also cook them in boiling water. Either way, they'll cook quickly, in just a few minutes. Using a slotted spoon, transfer them to a serving dish. Don't discard the liquid.

To make the sauce: Melt the butter in a frying pan over medium heat. Then add the sage and let that cook for a few seconds. Make a simple roux by whisking in the flour and cook until it's fully combined. Whisk in the chicken stock or water and bring it to a light simmer. Add the cooked tortellini and cook for a few minutes, just to bring everything together. The sauce will thicken and reduce a bit. When you're happy with it, you're good to go.

Serve the tortellini with the sauce and finish with a drizzle of balsamic vinegar.

SERVES 6

NICOLA THE ENTREPRENEUR

This could have been the story of a guy who went to New York and made a ton of money on Wall Street. Instead, it's the story of a guy who went back home to a dairy farm in Parma, to bale hay and learn how to make cows happy.

Nicola Bertinelli was studying for his MBA overseas, at Guelph University just outside of Toronto, when he got a call from his father, Giovanni. Giovanni was a dairy farmer who had taken the business over from his father.

After a lifetime of working the farm, Giovanni said to Nicola, "I'm tired and I'm ready to give up the business. Do you want it? Or should I sell it? Figure out what you want to do and let me know ASAP."

Now, Nicola had grown up on the farm so he knew what was involved. The life of a dairy farmer is 24/7. There are no days off, or spontaneous weekend trips to the beach, or stops on the way home to socialize at the bar. The cows need tending every day.

So he thought, and he consulted his professors, and he thought some more. And then Nicola went home to Parma to carry the family business over to another generation.

Giovanni was strictly a dairy farmer. He sold the milk his cows produced to a consortium of Parmigiano-Reggiano producers. But his son had other plans: At first Nicola continued to sell the milk, but held a little back. He found a space down the road and opened his own *caseificio* (cheese-making operation) to try his hand at making Parmigiano-Reggiano.

This was a big gamble. Parmigiano-Reggiano has to age for a minimum of twelve months in a cantina before it can be certified, so he had a wait a year to see if he had made the right choice.

Now, just to backtrack for a moment, Parmigiano-Reggiano was developed by monks in the thirteenth century, and the way it's made hasn't changed since then. It's only produced in this one area in the world: Parma, Reggio Emilia, Modena and a few other locations between the rivers Po and Reno. It is strictly monitored by a consortium, and it has to be tested and found to have certain characteristics before it gets the final DOP stamp to certify that it's the real thing.

The reason it's so region specific is the soil. As Nicola explained it to me, the character of the cheese is shaped by three specific bacteria that he calls "the three amigos." The valley in the Parma area produces alfalfa that contains these three living bacteria. Without getting too complicated, the alfalfa is harvested in the morning because that's when you know you're getting the three amigos. The alfalfa is then put into huge bales and fed to the cows. At every step—from the feeding to the milking through the cheesemaking process—everything is tested to make sure that the three amigos are alive and well.

Now back to Nicola's first batch of cheese. As it turns out, after the twelve-month aging period, his cheese got the stamp of approval as true Parmigiano-Reggiano. The family business had a new dimension.

Then the fun really started. Nicola opened a cheese shop to sell his cheese and a coffee bar to use his milk in cappuccino and pastries. From there, his business has grown to include a restaurant that turns into a nightclub complete with an outdoor poolside bar.

If Nicola regrets giving up the potential of a career on Wall Street for the life of a farmer, I couldn't see it. He is meticulous about every aspect of his business, and feels happy and blessed that he's putting a great product into the world and that he's found his calling in the family tradition.

Even Nicola's cows are happy. He wants them to be that way. They're kept in one of the cleanest barns I've ever seen, where in the hot summer months there's a constant mist to cool them down. Nicola says happy cows make better cheese.

PARMIGIANO CREAM CROSTINI

2 pears

2 tbsp (30 mL) extra-virgin olive oil

Freshly cracked black pepper, QB

1 lb (500 g) Parmigiano-Reggiano, finely grated

1 to 1 1/2cups (250 to 375 mL) dry white wine or extra dry prosecco

1 baguette, cut on the diagonal into 15 to 20 crostini

Aged balsamic vinegar, for drizzling

When I was hanging out with Nicola and his father, this was our go-to *aperitivo*. We'd always have it with a glass of prosecco or Lambrusco.

It's a simple recipe. The wine adds moisture to the grated Parmigiano, making it spreadable for your crostini. You can toast the crostini or not. If you want, you can eliminate the pear and mix the Parmigiano and wine with chopped walnuts and chopped black olives. Or add chopped sundried tomatoes to the mixture. But this is how we ate it.

Cube and finely dice the pears. (Leave skin on for texture.) Drizzle with olive oil and freshly cracked black pepper. Mix and set aside.

In a mixer, combine the Parmigiano-Reggiano and white wine and blend until well incorporated and creamy.

Spread on the crostini and top with pear mixture. Drizzle with balsamic vinegar. Serve immediately.

MAKES 15 TO 20 CROSTINI

PARMIGIANO-REGGIANO POTATOES

1 1/2 lb (750 g) Yukon Gold potatoes, peeled and chopped

3 sprigs fresh rosemary, needles only, roughly chopped

1/2 cup (125 mL) extra-virgin olive oil

Salt, QB

A good handful or two of freshly grated Parmigiano-Reggiano

I love roasted potatoes with rosemary. It's one of my favorite *contorni*, or sides. Adding Parmigiano to the equation is just taking something that's already perfect and making it that much better.

Preheat the oven to 400°F (200°C).

Put the potatoes in a roasting pan. Sprinkle with the rosemary, olive oil and salt and toss well. Make sure the potatoes are spread out in a single layer.

Roast the potatoes in the oven for about 35 minutes. When they've turned slightly golden, remove from the oven. Sprinkle with the Parmigiano and mix well. Put them back in the oven for another 10 minutes.

SERVES 4 TO 6

PARMIGIANO SALAD BASKETS

2 cups (500 mL) freshly grated Parmigiano-Reggiano

I love fried Parmigiano, or *frico* as they call it in Northern Italy. It's a fantastic cocktail snack served with a glass of prosecco. It's also a great snack for kids. I often put Parmigiano bites into salads to entice my children to eat more leafy greens.

The same technique that produces delicious *frico* from the grated Parmigiano makes these little baskets that I use to serve salads. As you eat the salad, you can break up the basket with your fork and get little Parmigiano chips as you go.

Get a cup or a small bowl to use as a mold for your baskets. Heat a small non-stick frying pan over high heat. Sprinkle 1/2 cup (125 mL) of the Parmigiano evenly over the bottom of the pan. Once the cheese melts, forming a thin wafer, remove the pan from the heat. Flip it over onto your inverted cup or bowl and, with your spatula, gently guide your cheese so that it falls onto the mold. As it cools, the cheese will solidify and form your basket.

Don't get hung up on whether or not they look perfect. They'll taste great either way.

MAKES 4 BASKETS

WINE-POACHED PEARS WITH PARMIGIANO AND RICOTTA

2 pears

2 cups (500 mL) dry white wine

1/3 cup (75 mL) granulated sugar

Pinch of saffron threads

Zest of 1 lemon

1/2 cup (125 mL) ricotta

1/2 cup (125 mL) finely grated Parmigiano-Reggiano

1 tsp (5 mL) ground cinnamon (optional)

1 tsp (5 mL) granulated sugar (optional)

Fruit, wine and cheese is a very typical Italian dessert. This is kind of a twist on that idea. When you poach the pears you get a chance to add more flavors—the combination of wine and saffron with a hint of lemon is slightly exotic. Parmigiano and ricotta are two of my favorite cheeses, and they complement the pear really well.

Cut the pears in half, remove the core and seeds and peel off the skin.

Heat the wine in a saucepan over medium-high heat. Stir in 1/3 cup (75 mL) sugar along with the saffron and lemon zest. Let it come to a boil. Once the sugar has dissolved, add the pears and cook for about 10 minutes, occasionally spooning some of the liquid over the pears. Turn the pears over and cook for another 10 minutes.

While the pears are poaching, combine the ricotta and Parmigiano in a bowl. Mix well. If you want, you can add some cinnamon or 1 tsp (5 mL) sugar, but I like the contrasting flavors of the sweet ricotta and the sharp, salty Parmigiano.

When the pears have finished poaching, remove them from the pan. Let the wine in the pan continue to cook until it is reduced by about two-thirds. You'll be left with a beautiful, thick syrup.

To serve, put a pear on a plate with a scoop of the Parmigiano and ricotta mixture, and drizzle with the wine reduction.

SERVES 4

CHOCOLATE PARMIGIANO NUGGETS

12 oz (375 g) Parmigiano-Reggiano

7 oz (200 g) bittersweet chocolate

When you're hanging out at Nicola's and you are surrounded by the best Parmigiano around, you're going to use just about any excuse to go into the kitchen and cook with it. And, honestly, I couldn't resist.

Late one night, Nicola and a few friends and I were sitting around the table after dinner, drinking red wine and talking. At Nicola's there's always Parmigiano at the table. Someone wanted chocolate, so Nicola brought some out, and pretty soon we were all eating both of them. I liked the way everything went together. So the next day I went into the kitchen and created this. It became the go-to late-night sweet bite for the rest of my stay.

Break the Parmigiano into chunks about the size of a walnut half.

Melt the chocolate in a double boiler (see page 152).

Using tweezer tongs, dip the little chunks of Parmigiano in the melted chocolate, coating the cheese completely. Immediately transfer them to a plate lined with waxed or parchment paper.

When you're done, put them in the fridge to cool. You can serve them directly from the fridge or let them come to room temperature.

MAKES ABOUT 24 NUGGETS

PATRIZIA THE HOSTESS

The Maremma district is on the southwestern tip of Tuscany and includes a rugged coastal area. It's a beautiful mix of land and sea, and I love going there.

For years I've been staying at the San Giusto Agriturismo run by Patrizia and her family. Patrizia does not run a glamorous agriturismo. It's a bit like staying at your grandmother's. Some of the furniture seems to be from the 1970s at best. But the hospitality and casual affection—and the pecorino cheese they make on the property—makes everything else seem unimportant.

There's a wonderful informality at Patrizia's. All the guests eat meals at the big harvest table with her family. You eat what the family eats. Just like home. Fortunately, they eat really well.

Patrizia's husband, Ovidio, and son, Federico, are known in the area for their sheep's milk cheese. They make some of the best ricotta that I've ever had. To wake up in the morning and have their warm fresh ricotta with a drizzle of olive oil on my bruschetta is a bit of heaven.

So at Patrizia's you may forgo the bells and whistles of a fancy agriturismo, but what you get in return is home-style hospitality and a feeling that you're part of the family, too.

COZZE GRATINATE

2 lb (1 kg) mussels, debearded and scrubbed

1/2 cup (125 mL) plain dry bread crumbs

1/2 cup (125 mL) freshly grated pecorino

1 bunch flat-leaf parsley, finely chopped

Salt, QB

Freshly ground black pepper, QB

2 tbsp (30 mL) extra-virgin olive oil (approx.)

The general rule of thumb in Italy is that you don't mix cheese with fish. But there are places, like the Maremma region, where that rule is relaxed, especially when using seafood like mussels.

This is a recipe Patrizia served me one evening. I loved it so much I made it the next day. In the Italian tradition of sharing recipes, she gave me the basics and I went at it.

These are great antipasti that you can serve warm or at room temperature.

Preheat your oven to 375°F (190°C).

To make the mussels: Pick over the mussels. Discard any that are open.

Put the mussels in a pot with a lid and add a couple of tablespoons (30 mL) of water. Steam them over high heat until they open (you can shake the pot a few times, if you want). This should only take 4 or 5 minutes. Discard any mussels that don't open. Let the mussels cool until you can handle them.

To make the filling: Mix together the bread crumbs, pecorino and parsley. Add salt and pepper to taste—be careful not to oversalt. Pour in just enough olive oil to bind the ingredients, and mix it together. You want a cohesive, but slightly loose, stuffing.

To put it all together: For each mussel, pull the mussel shells apart and discard the empty half of the shell. Generously top the other half with some of the bread crumb mixture and place it on a baking sheet. When you've filled them all, grate a little pecorino over top. Bake in the oven for 5 to 7 minutes, or until golden.

Let the cozze gratinate cool a bit before you dig in.

SERVES 4 TO 6

LAZY EGGPLANT PARMIGIANA

2 medium eggplants, cut lengthwise into thin slices

2 cups (500 mL) passata

Extra-virgin olive oil for drizzling

Salt, QB

2 sprigs fresh oregano

7 oz (200 g) pecorino, sliced

1 small bunch fresh basil, chopped

I'm Neapolitan. That means I love eggplant Parmigiana as much as I love getting my suit back from the tailor after he's adjusted it for me.

A true eggplant Parmigiano is a layered, cheesy, satisfying, beautiful dish that is as wonderful to anticipate as it is to eat. But, you know, I don't always have the time to go "full Parm." And sometimes I want the taste, but I don't want a heavy meal. After all, at Patrizia's there's cheesecake to come. So I've come up with what I call Lazy Eggplant Parmigiana.

What makes this lighter is that you're not frying your eggplant. And you top it with a little bit of tomato sauce and good pecorino cheese. That's it.

Make sure an oven rack is positioned in the top third of the oven, then preheat the oven to 350°F (180°C). Line a baking sheet with parchment paper.

To prepare the eggplant: Preheat your grill or a grill pan over high heat. Lightly char the eggplant slices on both sides. Place them in a single layer on the baking sheet.

To make the sauce: Heat the passata in a saucepan over medium heat. Add a drizzle of olive oil, some salt and the oregano and let it cook for about 5 minutes. You just want to warm the passata and let the flavors come together.

To assemble the dish: Spread the tomato sauce over the charred eggplant and top with slices of pecorino. Drizzle with some extra-virgin olive oil, if you want. Bake until the cheese melts and becomes slightly golden on top. Remove the pan from the oven and sprinkle the eggplant with the basil.

I'd let this sit a while so that you're not eating it piping hot out of the oven. Like traditional egg parm, I prefer to eat it a few hours after it has come out of the oven and has been resting at room temperature.

SERVES 4 TO 6

SPAGHETTI AL TONNO CON PECORINO

1 lb (500 g) spaghetti pasta

3 to 4 tbsp (45 to 60 mL) extra-virgin olive oil

1 clove garlic, finely chopped

2 tbsp (30 mL) capers, drained

2 cans (5 oz/150 g) tuna, drained and flaked

1/2 cup (125 mL) dry white wine

1/3 bunch fresh flat-leaf parsley, chopped

Salt, QB

Freshly ground black pepper, QB

1/2 cup (125 mL) finely grated pecorino, divided

1/2 cup (125 mL) plain dry bread crumbs, toasted

On the last day of my visit, Patrizia and I were sitting around talking, as usual. She jokingly suggested that I was living *la dolce vita* at her place and that maybe it was time I did some of the cooking! So here's what I made for her and her family.

The sauce cooks quickly, so get your pot of water on for your pasta.

Put a large pot of water on to boil. When the water boils, salt it and drop in the pasta. Give it a quick stir.

Heat a pan over medium heat. Add the olive oil, garlic and capers and cook until the garlic is soft but not brown. Add the tuna, breaking it up with your fork, and cook for about a minute. Add the white wine, parsley and salt and pepper, and cook until the wine is reduced by half.

Reduce the heat to low and let your sauce rest while your pasta finishes cooking.

When the spaghetti is moments away from being al dente, drain it, reserving about 1/2 cup (125 mL) of the cooking water.

Toss the cooked pasta in the sauce, along with the reserved water, and increase the heat to medium-high. Let the pasta finish cooking in the sauce for just a couple of minutes. The starches in the pasta water will help the sauce cling to the noodles.

Remove the pan from the heat, add half of the pecorino and toss it together.

Divide the pasta evenly among your serving plates. Finish each serving with the toasted bread crumbs and the remaining pecorino. Serve immediately.

SERVES 4 TO 5

PATRIZIA'S NO-BAKE CHEESECAKE

Crust

1 bag (10 oz/300 g) chocolate wafer cookies

1/4 cup (60 mL) butter, melted

Filling

2 sheets gelatin

Scant 1/4 cup (60 mL) milk

1 cup (250 mL) whipping (35%) cream

2 cups (500 mL) ricotta

1 cup (250 mL) plain yogurt

Bittersweet chocolate shavings, QB

This is a simple, lush, no-bake cheesecake that, aside from the cookies, contains no extra sugar. Because the ricotta is the star of this cheesecake, use the best and freshest you can find.

To make the crust: Crush the cookies. Patrizia's old-school technique was to just hand me a big metal bowl and get me to crush the cookies with my hands until they turned into crumbs. You could also bash them up a little with a rolling pin.

When the cookies are crushed, add the melted butter and mix well. Press the mixture evenly into the bottom of a 11- x 7-inch (28 x 18 cm) pan. Set aside.

To make the filling: Place the gelatin sheets in a small bowl of cold water and let them sit for about 10 minutes. Once they're softened, gently squeeze the soaked gelatin to remove excess water.

In a saucepan, bring the milk to a boil. Reduce the heat, add the gelatin and simmer, stirring, until it dissolves. Remove the pan from the heat and let it sit until it cools to room temperature.

In a bowl, with a whisk or an electric mixer, whip the cream until it's fluffy and stiff peaks form.

In a separate bowl, whip together the ricotta and the yogurt until smooth. Then fold in the whipped cream and milk mixture until it's combined.

Pour the cheese mixture over the crust. Shave chocolate over the top to completely cover. Let it sit in the fridge for 6 to 8 hours to set.

SERVES 8 TO 10

MAMMA E PAPÀ

My parents emigrated from Italy to Toronto. They worked hard, but they always knew how to have fun. And a lot of the fun—gatherings, celebrations, etc.—revolved around food. They ignited my passion for food and nurtured it, and I think it's safe to say that they're my biggest influences in that regard. And although I always loved what we made and ate at home, there was a time when I wasn't always so comfortable with the way "our food" worked in the outside world.

My school lunches were a daily dance with embarrassment. I'd open my bag to find an asiago, prosciutto and rapini sandwich on a crusty bun. What a nightmare. The kids would yell *"Eww!"* and ask me what the green stuff was. And I, feeling very different, yearned to open my lunch bag and find a peanut butter and jam sandwich on white bread.

And then there were the in-house incidents.

Some of the kids on our street had pet rabbits. We had pet rabbits, too. But ours landed on our table within six weeks. I remember having a friend over for dinner. He complimented my mother on the delicious chicken. Without blinking an eye my mom said, "It's not chicken. It's rabbit!" He started crying. I was humiliated.

Not all of the food-related incidents were so potentially traumatizing for the neighbors.

I remember a pivotal moment: One of the fathers was taking his son to the Royal Ontario Museum and he offered to take me, too. When the car pulled up, my mom walked me out and handed the dad a paper bag showing signs that something fried was inside. Was she *trying* to ruin my life? I wondered in deep humiliation. Inside the bag were potato croquettes. And as we drove, my friend and his dad started to eat them, saying things like "This is so delicious!" and "Can you believe she made these herself?" That was a turning point for me. I felt the humiliation lift and more than a little Italian family pride taking its place.

We were different. It may seem strange to say now, but when I was a kid, being Italian meant you sometimes faced discrimination. To a kid, fitting in is all that matters. And when it came to food, there was always something that underlined just how different you were. For instance, today you can get olive oil in most corner stores, but back when I was a kid, my grandmother used to have to go across town on the bus to one of the few stores that sold it. Then there were the family outings to pick wild dandelions that we cooked and ate. I prayed that none of the other kids would see my crazy immigrant family picking weeds. Or how about the way the zucchini farmer would give my mom the flowers for free? Here we were, eating food that other people were mowing down or giving away.

Sometimes things happened that made me cringe. But more and more as we were growing up, my parents would invite the neighbors over for dinner and I'd watch while they were blown away by the kind of food that we ate every day. That impressed me and made me proud. I learned at my family table that food had the power to bring people together and to make strangers into friends.

When you're the kid of Italian immigrants, you grow up eating what's put in front of you. You sit at the big table and are expected to just eat what they give you. Maybe as little kids we were accommodated a bit, but mostly we just ate. As a result, people thought we had sophisticated palates as kids. To me, it was just life in an Italian household.

For any Italian brought up in a traditional way, there are so many sense memories associated with cooking that follow you into your adult life. Every Italian grows up with the smell of a tomato sauce simmering away on the stove.

Today when I walk around the streets of Italy, and the same smells waft out of the little houses and apartments, I feel an incredible sense of nostalgia and love.

ANCHOVY MARINATA

1 lb (500 g) fresh anchovies

Salt, QB

White wine vinegar, QB

Extra-virgin olive oil, QB

1 bunch fresh flat-leaf parsley, chopped

1 cup (250 mL) whole black olives

Dried chili flakes, QB (optional)

Seafood is my dad's forte. That's because he grew up in the small town of Pozzuoli on the outskirts of Naples, where seafood is a big part of the diet.

In my family we always had anchovy marinata as an antipasto on Wednesdays. The fresh fish came into Toronto on Wednesday mornings, and my dad would go get some and we'd eat them that night. This recipe requires you to clean your anchovies. Don't get freaked out—anchovies aren't a messy fish to clean.

To clean the anchovies: There's nothing delicate about cleaning anchovies. You rip the heads off, gently pull the fish open and remove the spine. With your finger, scrape out the guts and rinse under cold running water.

Lay out the anchovy fillets on a plate. Season with salt and pour over just enough vinegar to cover them. Let them marinate for about 20 minutes or until the anchovies turn white.

Take the anchovies out of the vinegar and pat them dry with paper towels. Then lay them on a serving dish. Season with olive oil, parsley, olives and chili flakes.

You can make this recipe in advance and store it in a jar in the fridge. Just cover the anchovies with olive oil. They'll last a few weeks.

SERVES 4 TO 6

FRIED ANCHOVIES

2 lb (1 kg) fresh anchovies

All-purpose flour, QB

Extra-virgin olive oil, QB

If you want to get your kids to eat fish, I highly recommend making fried anchovies. My parents made them for us when we were kids, and now I do it for mine. My kids love them. Anchovies are a sweet fish, and these are delicate on the inside, crispy on the outside. They're small enough so that the kids can pick them up and eat them like finger food.

Clean and fillet the anchovies (see page 191), rinse them under cold running water and pat dry with paper towels.

Place the flour on a plate, then dredge the anchovy fillets in the flour, coating them completely.

Pour about 1/2 inch (1 cm) of olive oil into a frying pan and heat it over high heat. To test to see if the oil is hot, drop in a small bread cube or bread crumbs. If they fry immediately, you're good to go. Carefully drop the anchovies into the pan and fry until golden. They cook quickly, so work in batches and keep your eye on them.

Transfer the fried anchovies to a plate lined with paper towels to absorb any excess oil.

Serve.

SERVES 6 TO 8

David Rocco

SQUID FRITTERS

4 medium squid, cleaned

1 cup (250 mL) cubed salami

1/2 cup (125 mL) plain dry
bread crumbs

1/2 cup (125 mL) freshly grated
Parmigiano-Reggiano

1/2 cup (125 mL) extra-virgin
olive oil, divided, plus more as
needed

1/2 cup (125 mL) dry white
wine

1 large egg

1/2 bunch fresh flat-leaf
parsley, finely chopped

Salt, QB

Freshly ground black pepper,
QB

Semolina flour, QB

Clearly, I'm my mom's favorite. I'm the youngest of three. My mother's last child. My mama's baby boy. So how could I not be? One time, I was on my way to Florence to see my parents. Because I'm mom's favorite child, she always greets me by cooking something I love. Knowing I was coming off a long flight, she wanted to surprise me by making one of my favorites, stuffed calamari. I love this dish so much!

But on this particular morning when my dad went out to buy squid, they only had small ones. When my mom tried to stuff them, the squid fell apart. She was devastated that she couldn't make her baby his stuffed calamari. But being a good Italian cook, she never throws anything away. So she improvised.

Cut to that afternoon when I arrived. Mom was clearly upset. She told me that she had wanted to make a favorite dish for me, but it was a bit of a disaster. She apologized profusely. But when we got to the table and she served what she'd made from the ingredients—squid fritters—*O Dio!* One bite and they instantly went into my top-favorites-of-all-time column. Now I make these all the time for my family.

Roughly chop the squid and put them in a bowl. Add the salami, bread crumbs, Parmigiano, 1/4 cup (60 mL) olive oil, wine, egg and parsley and mix that all together. Add a pinch of salt and pepper and mix again. With your hands, shape golf ball–size chunks into patties.

In a separate dish, dredge the fritters in the semolina flour.

Heat up the remaining 1/4 cup (60 mL) of olive oil in a frying pan over high heat, and when the oil is hot fry the fritters on both sides until golden. If you need more oil, add a little more as needed. Remove to a plate lined with paper towels to absorb any excess oil, and serve.

SERVES 6 TO 8

SUMMERTIME MINESTRONE

1/4 cup (60 mL) extra-virgin olive oil, plus more for drizzling

2 carrots, diced

1 stalk celery, diced

1 large onion, finely diced

1 clove garlic, finely chopped

1 zucchini, diced

2 cups (500 mL) cooked cannellini beans (page 10) or 1 can (19 oz/ 540 mL) cannellini beans, rinsed and drained

1 bunch fresh spinach, trimmed and roughly chopped

1 bunch Swiss chard, trimmed and roughly chopped

Salt, QB

Freshly ground black pepper, QB

8 to 10 fresh basil leaves, roughly chopped

1/2 cup (125 mL) freshly grated Parmigiano-Reggiano

Minestrone is an iconic Italian dish, but its roots are in *cucina povera*. From such humble beginnings came one of the best soups in the world.

When I was little my grandmother would babysit me. I have memories of sitting at the kitchen table, eating my lunch and watching her through the window as she picked escarole, zucchini, carrots and potatoes from her garden. She'd come back, clean and peel the vegetables, and by the time we were done with lunch the minestrone would be simmering away on the stove, so it would be ready for our supper.

I don't call for stock. I use water because as you cook the vegetables the water becomes richly flavored. But if you have some on hand and want to use it, be my guest.

Heat the olive oil in a large pot over medium-high heat. When the oil shimmers, add the carrots, celery, onion and garlic. Cook until they soften and the onion becomes translucent. Then add the zucchini and cook until the zucchini softens. Add the beans and 5 cups (1.25 L) of water and bring to a boil. Reduce the heat to medium, add the spinach and Swiss chard and cook for about 45 minutes to an hour, depending on how you like the texture of your vegetables.

Turn off the heat. Add salt and pepper to taste, cover the pot with a lid and let it rest on the stove for another hour.

Just before serving, add the basil leaves and give it a good mix.

Drizzle each serving with olive oil and sprinkle with some Parmigiano.

SERVES 4 TO 6

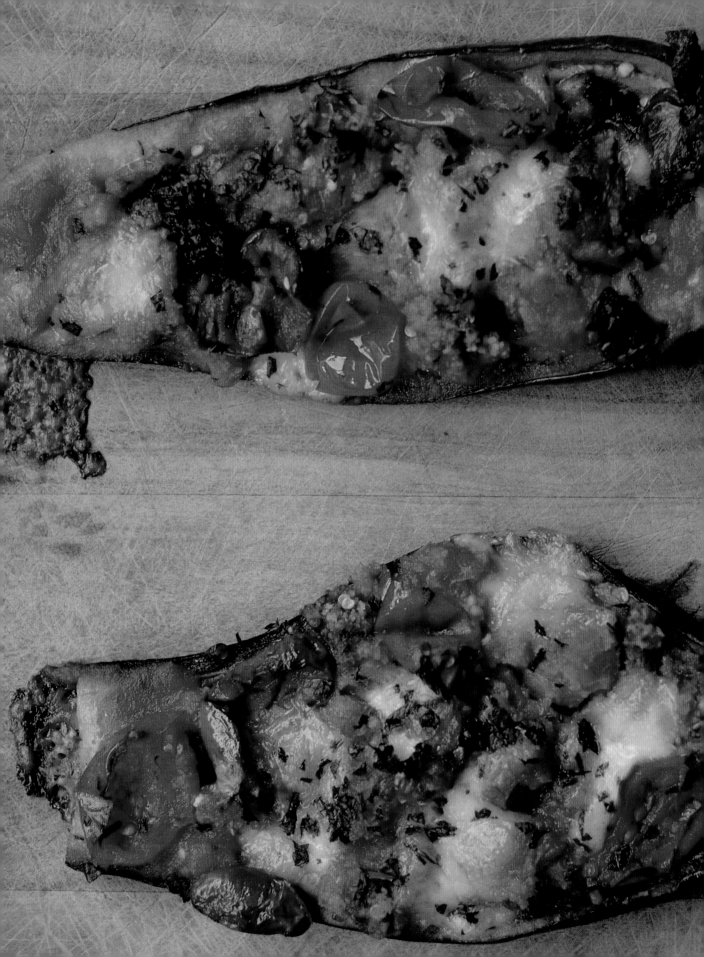

MELANZANE A BARCHETTA

3 Italian eggplants, halved lengthwise

1 pint (25 to 30) cherry tomatoes, halved lengthwise

10 green or black olives, pitted

2 to 3 tbsp (30 to 45 mL) capers, drained

1/3 cup (75 mL) to 1/2 cup (125 mL) extra-virgin olive oil, plus more for drizzling

1/2 cup (125 mL) passata

Salt, QB

Fresh oregano, chopped, QB

1 cup (250 mL) shredded mozzarella

1 cup (250 mL) shredded smoked scamorza

If you love eggplant, these stuffed and baked eggplants are delicious and really easy to make. My mom used to make extra because they taste even better the next day, even at room temperature.

Preheat your oven to 375°F (190°C).

Scoop the inside of the eggplant out, leaving a little bit of the flesh around the edges. You're going to stuff the filling back in, so you don't want the eggplants to fall apart when they cook. Arrange the eggplant shells, cut-side up, on a baking sheet and set aside.

Roughly chop the eggplant flesh and put it in a mixing bowl. Add the tomatoes, olives, capers and olive oil. Stir well.

Divide the filling into equal portions and fill each of the eggplant halves. Add a good drizzle of olive oil over each one. Spoon a little of the passata on each half, and add a pinch of salt and a sprinkle of fresh oregano. Top with mozzarella and scamorza.

Bake in the oven for about 45 minutes, until the eggplant is tender and the top is golden.

These beauties always taste better when they've been sitting for a while. The flavors intensify as they cool. So when they're done, I turn off the heat and let them rest in the oven for another hour and a half and then serve them at room temperature.

SERVES 4 TO 6

THE PALIO

Even in a country that is obsessed with tradition, the Palio stands out.

The Palio is a horse race that happens twice a year—in July, and then again in August—at the beautiful main Piazza del Campo in the ancient town of Siena. But it is so much more than a horse race. As someone said to me, "In Siena, the Palio is religion."

Years ago the city was divided up into *contrade,* or districts. There are currently seventeen of them. And you are born into yours. A *contrada* may have tens of thousands of people in it, but for the purposes of the Palio, these people are your family. For each and every person, winning the Palio is a goal so desired that it is hard to describe if you haven't experienced it.

In fact, the Palio is so deeply tied to tradition that for the five days leading up to the race, the entire city changes its character. Just to give you an idea: During those five days, couples in "mixed" marriages—i.e., from different *contrade*—don't sleep together. It's that intense.

This is an ancient tradition: The roots go back to medieval times. The modern Palio itself was first run in the mid-1600s. Since then it has been run every year, no matter what else has been going on in the world. Nothing, not even two world wars, have stopped the Palio.

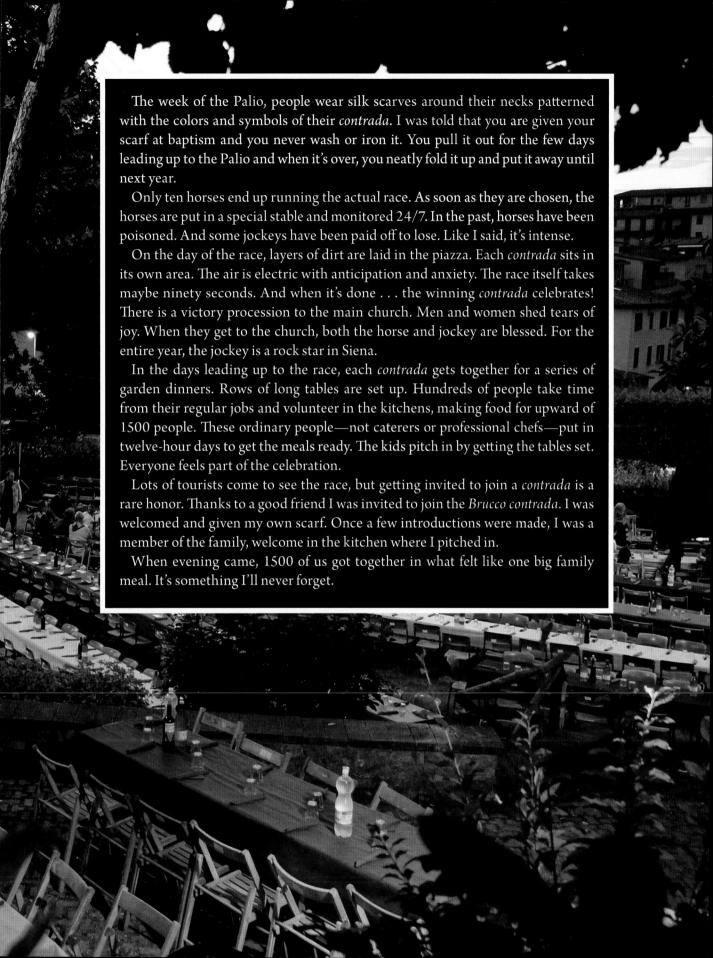

The week of the Palio, people wear silk scarves around their necks patterned with the colors and symbols of their *contrada*. I was told that you are given your scarf at baptism and you never wash or iron it. You pull it out for the few days leading up to the Palio and when it's over, you neatly fold it up and put it away until next year.

Only ten horses end up running the actual race. As soon as they are chosen, the horses are put in a special stable and monitored 24/7. In the past, horses have been poisoned. And some jockeys have been paid off to lose. Like I said, it's intense.

On the day of the race, layers of dirt are laid in the piazza. Each *contrada* sits in its own area. The air is electric with anticipation and anxiety. The race itself takes maybe ninety seconds. And when it's done . . . the winning *contrada* celebrates! There is a victory procession to the main church. Men and women shed tears of joy. When they get to the church, both the horse and jockey are blessed. For the entire year, the jockey is a rock star in Siena.

In the days leading up to the race, each *contrada* gets together for a series of garden dinners. Rows of long tables are set up. Hundreds of people take time from their regular jobs and volunteer in the kitchens, making food for upward of 1500 people. These ordinary people—not caterers or professional chefs—put in twelve-hour days to get the meals ready. The kids pitch in by getting the tables set. Everyone feels part of the celebration.

Lots of tourists come to see the race, but getting invited to join a *contrada* is a rare honor. Thanks to a good friend I was invited to join the *Brucco contrada*. I was welcomed and given my own scarf. Once a few introductions were made, I was a member of the family, welcome in the kitchen where I pitched in.

When evening came, 1500 of us got together in what felt like one big family meal. It's something I'll never forget.

PANZANELLA

12 thick slices of Tuscan-style bread

12 cherry tomatoes, halved lengthwise, or 6 field tomatoes, chopped

1 red onion, thinly sliced

6 fresh basil leaves, torn

Salt, QB

Freshly ground black pepper, QB

1/2 cup (125 mL) extra-virgin olive oil (or QB)

3 tbsp (45 mL) red wine vinegar

2 cans (5 oz/150 g) premium tuna (or QB) (optional)

One of the salads we made for 1500 people was *panzanella*. It's a classic salad that everyone in Tuscany has grown up eating. I often make this at home for my family. In fact, when the tomatoes are fresh and at their peak, and you can get your hands on freshly pressed olive oil, this is something we have three or four times a week.

In our household we have a little a problem. We rarely have any stale rustic bread. Between *scarpetta* and dipping bread into fresh olive oil for a snack, there's never any left over. And you can't use fresh bread for *panzanella*. It wouldn't work. So I cheat. I put the slices of bread in the oven and toast them. It's not traditional, but it works. The other nontraditional thing we sometimes do is add a few cans of tuna. Adding protein makes the salad more of a substantial meal. Everyone loves it. If you try it, you'll see why we eat this so much!

If you're using fresh bread, start by toasting it in the oven. Once it cools down, you can either cut it into small croutons or keep the bread whole and *quickly* submerge the slices in a bowl of water. And I really do mean *quickly* here. You do not want to turn your bread into a *pappa* or mush; the bread should still have some crunch to it. Then either rip the bread up or cut it with a knife.

Put the bread pieces in a large bowl. Add the tomatoes, onion, basil, salt, pepper, olive oil and red wine vinegar. Toss to combine.

Just a note here: I specify 1/2 cup (125 mL) of oil because if you're not used to making this dish, you might think that I was going overboard if I suggested more. But believe me, if you have good olive oil, you'll want to use more. We do.

If you want to add the tuna, flake it and add it to the bowl. Give it a good mix.

Let the whole thing rest for a half hour before you eat it.

SERVES 4

MY PALIO PASTA

6 stalks asparagus, cut into 1-inch (2.5 cm) pieces

1 cup (250 mL) fresh, canned (rinsed and drained) or frozen fava beans

1/4 cup (60 mL) extra-virgin olive oil

3 cloves garlic, smashed

5 oz (150 g) pancetta, cubed

1/2 tsp (2 mL) dried chili flakes

2 cups (500 mL) passata

Salt, QB

1 batch (500 g) Tuscan Pici (page 135)

1/2 cup (125 mL) freshly grated pecorino

I call this my Palio pasta because the week I was there I had this three times! I love asparagus, fava and pancetta (let's face it, pancetta makes everything taste better), and it's an unexpected combination in a pasta sauce.

Put a pot of water on to boil. When it boils, salt it. Add the asparagus and fava beans. If you want, you can put the asparagus and beans in a metal strainer and lower that into the pot. It's easier to pull them out that way. Cook the asparagus and beans for about 5 minutes. I like mine to have a bit of bite, but I'll leave that to you. Remove them and set aside.

At this point you can either keep this water boiling or you can drain it and put a new batch of water on to boil. Either way, you'll need boiling water for when it's time to cook your pasta.

Heat the olive oil in a sauté pan over medium heat. Add the garlic, pancetta and chili flakes and cook until the garlic is slightly golden and the pancetta is crispy. Add the cooked asparagus and fava beans, toss to combine and cook in the delicious rendered fat of the pancetta for a few minutes. Pour in the passata and stir. Add a dash of salt.

Toss the pici into the pot of boiling water. Since the pici is fresh, it will cook quickly, in 2 to 3 minutes. When the pasta rises to the surface, it's done.

Drain the pasta, reserving about 1/4 cup (60 mL) of the pasta cooking water.

Remove the garlic cloves from the sauce; they've done their job. Add the cooked pici along with the reserved pasta cooking water to the sauce and toss for 20 to 30 seconds to combine. Remove from heat and top with freshly grated pecorino.

Serve immediately.

SERVES 4

PANFORTE

1 cup (250 mL) figs, finely chopped

2/3 cup (150 mL) dates, pitted, finely chopped

1/2 cup (125 mL) liquid honey

1/2 cup (125 mL) packed brown sugar

1/2 tsp (2 mL) ground cinnamon

1/2 tsp (2 mL) ground cardamom

1/2 tsp (2 mL) ground cloves

1/2 tsp (2 mL) ground nutmeg

1/2 tsp (2 mL) freshly ground black pepper

1/4 cup (60 mL) roughly chopped bittersweet chocolate

2/3 cup (150 mL) candied orange rinds

2/3 cup (150 mL) candied lemon rinds

1/3 cup (75 mL) candied ginger

1/2 cup (125 mL) blanched almonds

1/2 cup (125 mL) hazelnuts, toasted

1/2 cup (125 mL) almonds, toasted

1/4 cup (60 mL) all-purpose flour, sifted

1 shot glass (1 1/2 oz/45 mL) Vin Santo or sweet port wine

Icing sugar, for dusting

The origin of this treat is a bit murky, but the consensus seems to be that it was in Siena sometime in the 1200s. And if you go to Siena, you'll see *panforte* in every sweet shop and every bar. As with any traditional Italian recipe, everyone has adapted it to their own taste—or their own *contrada*'s taste.

In fact, there's a school of thought that says *panforte* should have exactly seventeen ingredients for the seventeen *contrade* of the Palio.

The first time I tried *panforte*, I was taken aback by all the spices. The combination of flavors was not something I was used to, certainly not what you'd normally find in Italian sweets. But now that I'm older, I've come to really enjoy the taste. A little piece is all you need to satisfy that mid-afternoon sweet craving.

Preheat your oven to 325°F (160°C). Line a 9- by 5-inch (23 x 12.5 cm) loaf pan with parchment paper.

Put the figs and dates in a saucepan with just enough water to cover them. Then add the honey, brown sugar, spices and chocolate. Cook over medium-low heat, stirring, until the honey, sugar and chocolate are melted and the spices are dissolved. Scrape the mixture into a mixing bowl.

Add the candied fruit, nuts, flour and Vin Santo or port and stir everything together.

Scrape the mixture into the prepared loaf pan and bake for 35 to 40 minutes, until soft but firm. Don't overcook it!

Remove the pan from the oven and let it cool completely. Once cool, invert it onto a serving plate and pull off the parchment paper. Dust it generously with icing sugar.

It's rich and decadent, just as you'd expect from a taste of Siena. A small slice goes a long way.

MAKES ONE 9- X 5-INCH (23 X 12.5 CM) LOAF CAKE

THE WHEAT HARVEST

Just outside of Florence is a little town called Vicchio.

Every year they have a *festa* to mark La Battitura del Grano—the threshing of the wheat. The purpose is to celebrate the harvest and show the younger generation how things were done in the good old days. Mostly, I suspect, it's an opportunity for the farmers to get together with old friends and family and have a meal.

The men, who when I was there were in their eighties and nineties, were old enough to remember when doing *la battitura* was a heavy-duty, labor-intensive job.

They would beat the wheat with a heavy stick until the grain separated from the stalk. The grain was then collected and would be further cleaned by being tossed on a giant flat sieve.

When the threshing machine was invented, the local area could afford only one, and it would go from farm to farm during the harvest, with everyone waiting their turn. You can see how that would bring the community together and lead to a big party.

Of course, threshing machines have become more sophisticated. And even though threshing is not nearly as demanding these days, farming is still hard work. I'm someone who loves pasta and good bread, and attending the *festa* renewed my respect and appreciation for farmers everywhere.

CROSTINI TOSCANI

1 lb (500 g) chicken livers

1/4 cup (60 mL) extra-virgin olive oil

1 small red onion, finely chopped

1 medium carrot, finely chopped

1 medium stalk celery, chopped

1 tsp (5 mL) salt

1/2 cup (125 mL) Vin Santo

1 1/2 tbsp (17 mL) capers, drained

5 anchovy fillets, minced

1/2 cup (125 mL) chicken stock

1 Italian baguette, cut on the diagonal into 1/4- or 1/2-inch (0.5 to 1 cm) slices

Growing up, I wasn't a big liver fan. When my mom would make liver and onions, I'd try to outsmart my parents by hiding the liver under the onions. Strangely enough, I like eating these Tuscan crostini.

When I'm in Florence, this is one of those snacks I routinely have with a nice glass of chianti. Adding a little hit of Vin Santo to the crostini before you serve them gives the earthy liver a nice sweet flavor.

Prepare your chicken livers: Rinse them under cold running water and pat dry. Take a small knife and cut off any connective tissue and discard.

Now you're going to make a basic soffritto: Heat the olive oil in a frying pan over medium heat. Add the onion, carrot and celery and cook until the vegetables soften and the onion is translucent. Add the chicken livers and salt, and cook for 5 to 7 minutes, until the chicken livers are cooked through. Then stir in the Vin Santo, capers and anchovies and cook until the Vin Santo reduces a bit. Add the chicken stock and cook until almost all the liquid has evaporated and the chicken livers are soft and tender.

Turn off the heat and let the pan sit on the burner until the mixture cools to room temperature, to give the flavors a chance to come together. Then pour everything into a food processor and purée until smooth.

Serve with toasted crostini or bruschetta, and finish with a few drops of Vin Santo. *Da Dio!*

SERVES 8 TO 10

DUCK PASTINA SOUP

1 medium duck

1 tbsp (15 mL) coarse sea salt

1 large onion, halved

1 large carrot, roughly chopped

2 stalks celery, with leaves, roughly chopped

3 cloves garlic (unpeeled)

1 bunch fresh flat-leaf parsley

2 sprigs fresh rosemary

2 bay leaves

1 tsp (5 mL) black peppercorns

1 cup (250 mL) pastina pasta

2 eggs, beaten

1/2 cup (125 mL) freshly grated Parmigiano-Reggiano

Duck soup is a must during the *battitura*. Because it's a fatty soup, it soothes the farmers' throats from all the dust they take in during the threshing of the wheat. But even if you haven't spent the day threshing wheat, it's a really delicious soup.

I cook the duck on its own for about half an hour so that the fat and and any scum can be skimmed off fairly simply before you add the aromatics. You can, of course, make this with chicken.

Wash the duck well and cut it into 8 pieces. Put it in a big soup pot and pour in enough cold water to cover it by at least 1 inch (2.5 cm). Add salt.

Bring it to a boil, reduce the heat to medium and simmer for about 30 minutes, using a spoon to remove any scum and foam from the top of the water while it's cooking.

Add the vegetables, herbs and peppercorns. Cook for 2 more hours at a good simmer. The duck should always be well covered with water, so if you need to, add a little more water as you go, a cup or two (250 to 500 mL) at a time. Check the pot every so often, and if more scum or foam rises to the surface, remove it.

When it's done, remove the duck from the pot and set aside. Using a fine-mesh sieve, strain the broth into a clean pot and discard the solids. If you're going to make the tagliatelle (page 221), reserve 1/2 cup (125 mL) of the broth and set aside.

When the duck is cool enough to handle, pick off the meat and discard the fat and bones. Shred the meat.

Add some of the duck meat (QB) to the soup, and increase the heat to high. When the soup comes to a boil, add the pastina and give it a quick stir. Cook for about 7 minutes. Taste, and adjust the seasonings if you want. When the pasta is done, turn off the heat.

In a small bowl, whisk together the egg and Parmigiano. Slowly mix this mixture into the soup. Let it sit for 90 seconds so the egg cooks, then serve.

SERVES 6 TO 8

TAGLIATELLE WITH DUCK RAGÙ

1/4 cup (60 mL) extra-virgin olive oil, plus more for drizzling

1 red onion, minced

1/2 tbsp (7 mL) tomato paste

1 glass red wine (preferably Sangiovese)

Leftover cooked duck breast meat, QB, from Duck Pastina Soup (page 218)

1/2 cup (125 mL) reserved broth from Duck Pastina Soup (page 218)

1 lb (500 g) tagliatelle pasta

2 tbsp (30 mL) unsalted butter

1/2 cup (125 mL) freshly grated Parmigiano-Reggiano

This pasta course is perfect after duck soup (see page 218) since it can be made with the leftover meat. Duck meat is rich and fatty, and tastes delicious over a homemade fresh pasta like tagliatelle.

Put a large pot of water on to boil to cook your pasta. By the time the water starts boiling, the sauce will pretty much be ready.

Heat the olive oil in a frying pan over medium heat. Add the onion and cook until soft and translucent. Add the tomato paste, red wine and as much leftover duck as you'd like. Mix it together and cook until the wine reduces by about two-thirds. Then add the duck broth and let it cook down a bit.

Salt the boiling water in the pot and drop in the tagliatelle. When your pasta is almost al dente, drain it, reserving 1/4 cup (60 mL) of the pasta cooking water.

Add the cooked pasta to the pan with the duck ragù along with the reserved pasta cooking water. Toss to combine. Cook until the sauce has thickened a little. Stir in the butter and then the Parmigiano.

Serve the pasta with a drizzle of olive oil to finish.

SERVES 6

FARMER'S FRIED CHICKEN

1/4 cup (60 mL) extra-virgin olive oil

Juice of 2 lemons

4 cloves garlic, smashed

4 sprigs fresh rosemary

Salt, QB

Freshly ground black pepper, QB

1 whole chicken, cut into 8 pieces

Extra-virgin olive oil or vegetable oil, for frying

1 cup (250 mL) chickpea flour

Sparkling water, as needed

I love fried chicken. Who doesn't? But let's face it, it's all about the contrast between the really crispy coating and the juicy chicken. I got this recipe from one of the farmer's wives during a dinner. She called it Pollo Fritto al Contadino (Farmer's Fried Chicken). It has some classic Tuscan herbs, and my favorite thing is that it uses a chickpea flour that when fried gives it a nice crunchy exterior. After making it her way, I won't go back to any other recipe.

In a large bowl, put the olive oil, lemon juice, garlic, rosemary, salt and pepper and mix well. Then add the chicken pieces and toss to coat. If you want, you can also do this in a resealable bag. Put it in the fridge for about 90 minutes to marinate.

Pour about 1/2 to 1 inch (1 to 2.5 cm) of olive oil or vegetable oil into a deep frying pan and heat it over medium-high heat. (Alternatively, you can use a deep fryer, if you have one.)

Remove the chicken from the fridge and discard the marinade.

Pour the chickpea flour into a bowl. Add just enough sparkling water to make a thick, pancake-like batter. Add a pinch of salt and pepper, and stir well.

Dip the chicken into the batter, coating well. Then carefully place the coated chicken into the hot oil and fry on all sides until crisp and golden (10 to 15 minutes depending on the size of your pieces). When they're done, transfer the chicken to a plate lined with paper towels to absorb any excess oil.

Now, you can eat these as is and they'll be good. But if you like a really crisp coating, like the kind you'd find in a restaurant, you can fry them a second time, just for a few minutes. (This also works really well if you plan to make a big batch of this and serve it at a large party. Just reheat the oil before serving and refry the chicken.)

SERVES 4

PITIGLIANO

Pitigliano is a tiny Tuscan town of less than 5000 people located about midway between Siena and Rome. Seeing it for the first time is like encountering something out of a medieval dream.

As you're driving through the rolling hills of the Tuscan countryside, you turn a corner and suddenly you see an ancient town perched on a cliff. It's breathtaking.

Pitigliano has a colorful history that dates back to the Etruscans. It once had a thriving Jewish community and was nicknamed "Little Jerusalem." There is no Jewish community there any more, but the local residents are very proud of the Jewish influence on the life and cuisine of the city, as I discovered when one of the local chefs gave me a personal tour.

BUGLIONE D'AGNELLO

3 tbsp (45 mL) extra-virgin olive oil

4 cloves garlic (unpeeled)

2 sprigs fresh rosemary

2 lb (1 kg) lamb shoulder or neck, cut into chunks

1/2 cup (125 mL) white wine vinegar

1 cup (250 mL) dry white wine

1 tsp (5 mL) salt

1 tsp (5 mL) freshly ground black pepper

1/2 tsp (2 mL) dried chili flakes

2 cups (500 mL) vegetable stock

1/4 cup (60 mL) tomato paste

4 to 6 slices Tuscan-style bread

Chef Domenico of the restaurant Il Tufo Allegro took me for a walk to show me some of the historic sites that commemorate the Jewish history of Pitigliano. Then we headed back to his restaurant to make a Jewish dish that dates back to the 1500s. Like so many of my favorite recipes, this one uses "inferior" cuts of meat, like the shoulder and the neck, and lets slow cooking tenderize and bring out the best in them.

_____

In a Dutch oven or large heavy-bottomed pot, heat the olive oil, garlic (with the skin on or, as the Italians say, *in camicia*) and rosemary over high heat. Cook for about 30 seconds. Then add the lamb and sear on all sides until the meat develops a little crust. Add the vinegar, and cook for a minute. (Years ago the vinegar was used because some of the meats that were sold to Jewish people were not the best cuts, so the vinegar would take away the smell and reduce the gaminess. Today it's used to add flavor, but it also works to take away some of lamb's natural gaminess.)

Now, pour in the white wine. That will deglaze the pan and pick up all those bits of flavor that are stuck to the bottom. While the wine is doing its thing, sprinkle in the salt, pepper and chili flakes. Pour in the vegetable stock, put a lid on the pot, reduce the heat to medium-low and let it cook for half an hour.

Add the tomato paste and give it a little stir. Put the lid back on and cook for another hour.

Turn off the heat and let it sit for half an hour.

Serve over Tuscan bread.

SERVES 4 TO 6

EVERYBODY LOVES RAIMONDO

Raimondo is a Neapolitan chef now living in Tuscany. And the translation, for those of you who don't know your Italian stereotypes, is that Raimondo is a man of great exuberance, living in a quieter, more philosophically oriented part of the country.

So cooking with Raimondo was a noisy affair, with lots of verbal sparring about the right way to do pretty much everything. And that's less about him being a perfectionist than it is about him wanting to make sure everything he serves is, um, perfect. But that's because cooking and taking good care of his customers is his passion.

Raimondo's passing that passion on to his family. When I visited him, Raimondo's twelve-year-old grandson was already working in the restaurant, picking up his grandfather's energetic way of making sure every customer felt well taken care of.

Now, no self-respecting Neapolitan is ever going to abandon all the incredible food that Naples has given the culinary world, so Raimondo does what he calls Neapolitan-Tuscan fusion.

We made a variety of dishes and then ate them together, still arguing, on the small terrace of his restaurant—just twenty seats—overlooking the beautiful town of Pitigliano.

ACQUACOTTA

4 to 6 cups (1 to 1.5 L) water or vegetable stock

1 bunch chicory, chopped

2 cups (500 mL) shredded cabbage

2 large carrots, thinly sliced

1 onion, sliced

Salt, QB

Freshly cracked black pepper, QB

4 to 6 eggs (1 egg per person; optional)

4 to 8 slices day-old Tuscan-style bread (1 to 2 slices per person), toasted

Extra-virgin olive oil, for drizzling

I wonder what an eighteenth-century Italian peasant would make of what's happened to this dish. This is a soup that was originally made when there was very little available. Nothing to make stock from. Probably very few vegetables around, and the ones they had were wilting. From these extremely humble beginnings, *acquacotta*, which means "cooked water," has become something you can find on the menus of upscale trattorias. Oh, the irony.

If you want to turn this soup into a main, you can add an egg, as we've done here. You can also make this with vegetable stock.

Put the water or stock in a large pot and bring to a boil. Add all of your vegetables, and then reduce the heat to a simmer and cook until the carrots are soft. Taste the soup and QB your salt and pepper.

Crack the eggs into the simmering soup and cook until they are poached.

To serve, place a slice of crostini in the bottom of each soup bowl. With a slotted spoon, divide the vegetables and eggs among the bowls. Pour in as much of the broth as you'd like. Finish with some freshly cracked black pepper and a drizzle of olive oil.

SERVES 4 TO 6

PASTA WITH EGGPLANT AND BUFFALO MOZZARELLA

1/2 cup (125 mL) olive oil for frying

1 large eggplant, cubed

1 can (28 oz/796 mL) peeled whole plum tomatoes

3 tbsp (45 mL) extra-virgin olive oil

1 small onion, finely chopped

Salt, QB

Freshly ground black pepper, QB

1 batch (500 g) Fresh Pasta Dough (page 13)

1 large ball fior di latte, cubed

1/4 cup (60 mL) grated pecorino

6 basil leaves, torn

This dish is a Neapolitan classic. Growing up, I loved it. It's not generally something you'd find on a Tuscan menu, but with Raimondo's Neapolitan background, there it was.

Italy is very regional, and at times the locals can be food snobs (i.e., their region's food is supreme and everyone else's is inferior). When I'm in Italy shooting my TV show, my crew is all Tuscan and I'm the only Southern Italian. So when Raimondo and I fed this dish to my sometimes snobbish crew, it was a great pleasure to watch as they literally licked their plates clean. *Ahh,* sweet redemption.

When it comes to the pasta, this sauce is very democratic. It works really well with a thick, rustic pasta like Tuscan Pici (page 135), maltagliati, strozzapreti or even the Neapolitan scialatielli pasta.

Eggplant is like a sponge when it comes to oil. The way to make sure your eggplant fries without turning into an oil-soaked mess is to make sure the oil is extremely hot before you start frying. So, heat up 1/2 cup (125 mL) oil in your frying pan over high heat until it's just about smoking. Then cook the eggplant in batches, being careful not to crowd the pan. When it's golden, transfer to a plate lined with paper towels to absorb any excess oil.

Put a large pot of water on the stove for cooking your pasta and let it come to a boil while you're making your sauce.

Pour the tomatoes into a bowl and crush them with your hands. This way you can control the chunkiness of your sauce.

In a frying pan large enough to hold all of the ingredients, heat up 3 tbsp (45 mL) olive oil over medium heat. Add the onion and sauté until soft and slightly translucent. Add the crushed tomatoes, and a little salt and pepper, and let the whole thing simmer for about 5 minutes while you cook your pasta.

Salt your boiling water, drop in your pasta and give it a little stir. Fresh pasta cooks fast, in 2 to 3 minutes. When it rises to the surface, it's done. Drain the pasta.

Add the pasta and the eggplant to the tomato sauce and mix everything together. Take the pan off the heat. Add the fior di latte, pecorino and basil and stir to combine.

Serve immediately.

SERVES 4 TO 6

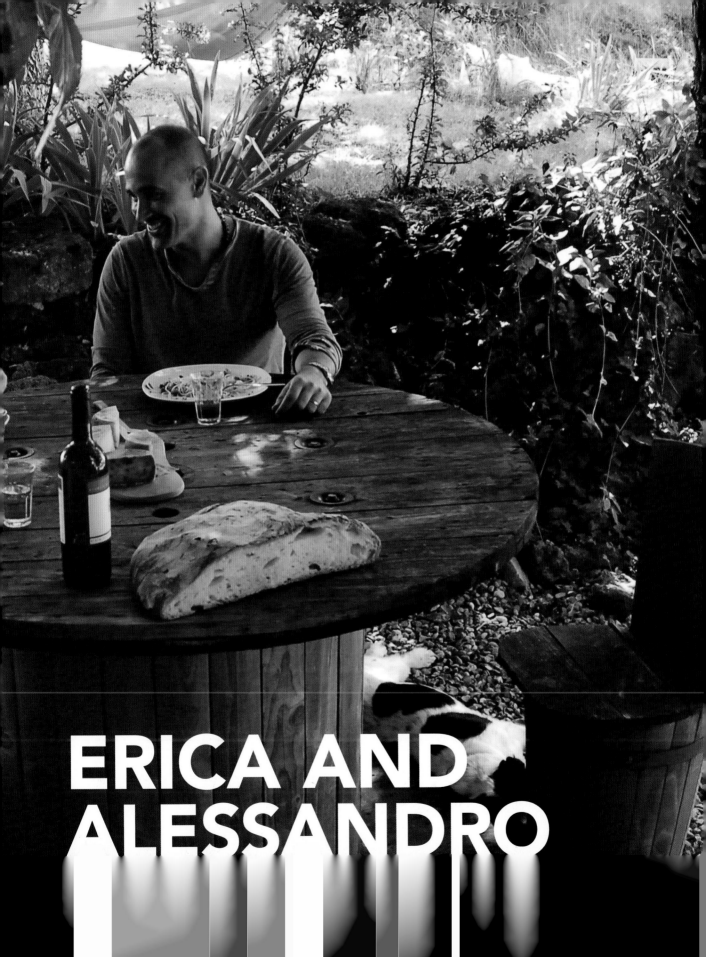

ERICA AND ALESSANDRO

Now this, to me, sounds like a storybook childhood. Erica's grandparents had an organic farm in the Chianti area, where she spent her weekends and summers. Her Nonno Nanni taught Erica how to cultivate the land and make good olive oil and good wine. He taught her how to take care of chickens, rabbits and pigeons. Her Nonna E would take her into the garden to see what was ready to be picked, then together they'd go into the kitchen and make traditional Tuscan *cucina povera* dishes—cooking only by the seasons—as well as jams, pies and bread.

But childhood ends, and Erica found herself working in the city of Florence. She married Alessandro, and they had busy city lives. After a few years, Erica and Alessandro had had enough. They decided that if they could find the right place, they'd open up an agriturismo and leave city life behind. Erica began the search. She spent three years looking before she found Sant'Egle, which is very close to Pitigliano. It was, says Erica, "love at first sight." The air was clear, you could hear birds singing and there was wildlife in the area. There was land for a garden. And there was even a connection to history—a building that dated back to the Etruscan era. It was just far enough from main roads to be quiet, but close enough so they could run a business. She and Alessandro took the biggest gamble of their lives: They sold everything and bought the place so they could live what they truly loved—a life in tune with nature—and offer that experience to others.

Sant'Egle is a completely organic farm. They practice a form of Japanese agriculture called *Fukuoka*, a sustainable, aesthetically beautiful style of gardening that she describes as "organic, synergistic farming . . . the art of cultivating, without torturing the land." Erica and Alessandro grow fruits, vegetables, saffron, spirulina and truffles. They use the produce to create menus for their guests. They are not trained chefs, but passionate, knowledgeable and talented cooks, who turn out beautiful Tuscan dishes, sometimes with a little twist. They know how to have fun with their excellent ingredients.

It's a life lived in tune with nature, and filled with kindness and generosity. "If you love the country life," says Erica, "it's a drastic, happy choice. Here, we are happy every day. The nature, the good food, the air, the seasons, are a gift that manifests itself every morning when we look out the window."

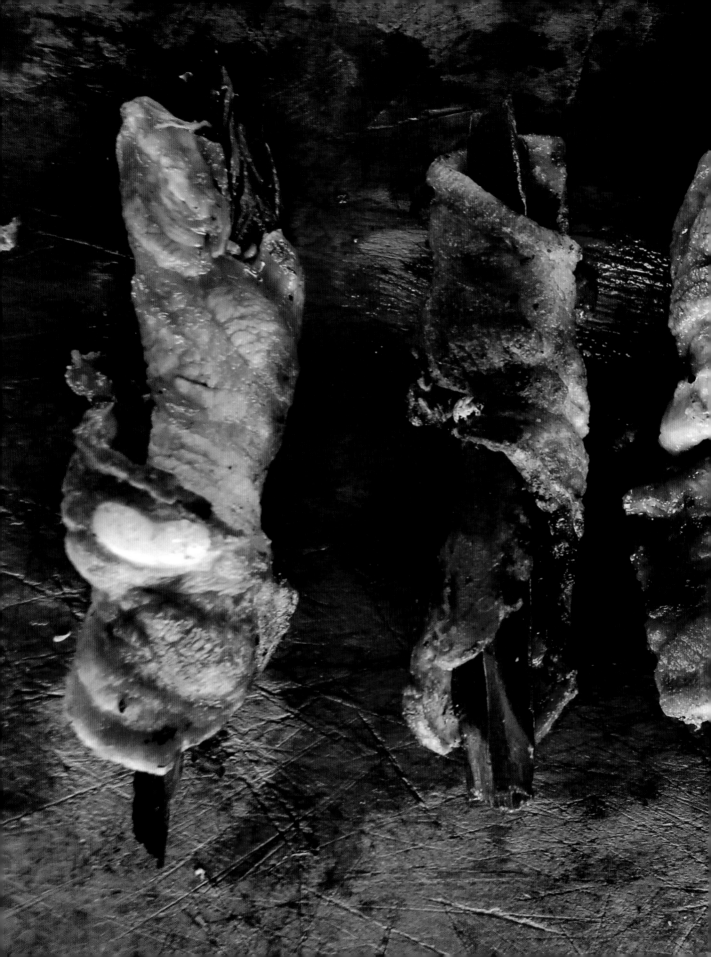

PANCETTA-WRAPPED LEEKS

Leeks, QB

Thickly cut slices pancetta, QB (1 slice per leek)

This was fun. Alessandro, Erica and I sat around an open fire, and they brought out some freshly picked leeks.

Most recipes call for using only the white part of the leek. This one uses only the green stem.

Wash the leeks well. Cut the white bulb-ends off and set aside for another use. Get sharp sticks or skewers and run one lengthwise through each green leafy stalk. Wrap the pancetta around the stalks, and cook over the barbecue or roast over an open fire, turning them every so often, until the pancetta is golden brown and crispy on all sides. Remove from the skewers and serve immediately.

SERVES AS MANY AS YOU LIKE

Dolce Famiglia

SPAGHETTI AGLIO E OLIO WITH WILD FENNEL

Wild fennel grows all over the Tuscan countryside, but I encountered it for the first time when I was visiting Alessandro and Erica. I really enjoyed it. Instead of being overly licoricey, like the fennel I'm used to, wild fennel is floral, with a delicate taste that hints of chamomile.

This recipe is a twist on the classic Aglio e Olio. I'm giving it to you as we made it, knowing that it may be difficult for you to source wild fennel. It's so interesting, and since it often happens that rare ingredients can suddenly become accessible, I want to share it.

This recipe calls for 2 tsp (10 mL) of wild fennel seeds. This refers to the flowery tops of the plant. You just rub the flowers between your fingers to get a mix of flowers and seeds that you can use in this dish.

If you can't find wild fennel, you can make this as a simple Aglio e Olio with croutons, which is incredibly delicious on its own. Or you can use regular fennel fronds. The taste won't be the same as this dish, but if you like fennel it's another interesting twist on this Italian classic.

---

1 lb (500 g) spaghetti pasta

3 tbsp (45 mL) extra-virgin olive oil

4 oz (125 g) dry bread, cut into cubes for croutons

Pinch of salt

3 cloves garlic, chopped

1/2 tsp (2 mL) dried chili pepper flakes

2 tsp (10 mL) wild fennel seeds (flowery tops)

1 small bunch wild fennel

1/2 cup (125 mL) freshly grated pecorino

Extra-virgin olive oil, for drizzling

Put a large pot of water on to boil. The water will likely come to a boil while you're making the sauce. Try to time this so the pasta comes out of the pot just when you're ready to add it to the sauce. When the water boils, salt it, drop in the pasta and give it a little stir. Cook it until it's slightly pre–al dente. Then drain it, reserving about 1 cup (250 mL) of the pasta cooking water.

Pour the olive oil in a frying pan over high heat. When the oil shimmers, add the bread cubes and a pinch of salt, and toss for a couple of minutes until the bread is crispy and golden. Transfer the croutons to a dish and set aside.

In the same frying pan, over medium-low heat, add the garlic and cook for about a minute. Stir in the chili flakes and wild fennel seeds and cook for about 30 seconds. Be careful here: You don't want to cook the garlic or fennel too fast. Your goal is to coax the sweetness out of the garlic; if it burns it will turn bitter. Add the croutons and cook for about a minute.

Add the cooked spaghetti, along with 1/2 cup (125 mL) of the reserved pasta cooking water, and cook for about a minute. If it's dry, avoid the temptation to add more oil. Add the remaining 1/2 cup (125 mL) of the reserved pasta cooking water instead. You want the pasta to finish cooking in the sauce and the flavors to mingle.

Rip some wild fennel tops off of the stems and sprinkle over the dish. Then add the pecorino.

Serve immediately, drizzled with some olive oil.

SERVES 4

SAFFRON TIRAMISÙ

5 egg yolks, preferably organic

1/3 cup (75 mL) organic cane sugar

Pinch of saffron threads

1 lb (500 g) mascarpone

1 to 2 cups (250 to 500 mL) cold brewed espresso

20 Italian ladyfinger cookies (preferably Pavesini or Savoiardi)

Tiramisù might be Italy's most famous dessert. And aside from the fact that it is delicious, it's also easy to make, no baking required. If you think of tiramisù as a heavy, whipped cream–filled cake, then I'm going to change your mind with this recipe.

Working with Erica reminded me of how simple and wonderful this classic is at its most basic. It doesn't need to be drowned in espresso for it to work, and there's no alcohol because it doesn't need it. In a way, it's a perfect metaphor for how Erica and Alessandro live.

Erica and Alessandro grow saffron on their property, so she adds some, which gives the dessert a beautiful color and adds a subtle flavor. But you can make this with or without the saffron. It's your choice. The only thing I'd recommend is that you use organic eggs and the best mascarpone you can get your hands on. You'll be impressed by how delicious it is. In fact, I sometimes just stop after blending the eggs, sugar and mascarpone, and serve that in a martini glass topped with berries.

In a mixing bowl, combine the egg yolks and sugar, and whisk until the sugar has dissolved and the yolks have turned a cream color. You can whisk this by hand or use an electric mixer if you want. Sprinkle in the saffron and mix gently.

In another bowl, whisk the mascarpone until loose and creamy. Fold the mascarpone into the egg and sugar mixture. Set aside.

Fill a separate bowl with the espresso. Quickly dip each biscuit into the bowl. You want the biscuits to absorb some of the coffee for flavor, but you don't want to drench them so they lose their integrity. I like the biscuit to have coffee flavor but still be firm.

I like to serve my tiramisù in individual glasses. I've used martini glasses or regular short drinking glasses. If you go that route, line the bottom of each glass with the dipped biscuits. Top with a big spoonful of the cream. If you want, do another layer. Refrigerate for at least an hour before serving.

SERVES 8 TO 10

SUMMER CAMP

For fifteen years now, my sister Maria has run an international summer camp in Magliano in Toscana, which is two and a half hours southwest of Florence. She hosts kids in a 300-year-old house called Il Capitana. It's on a beautiful piece of land surrounded by vineyards, olive groves, and vegetable and herb gardens.

The camp is called Canadian Island. The interesting thing about this is that there is no such thing as summer camp in Italy. Maria has taken the North American tradition and set it up in Italy, and she's been able to grow it over the years.

Like any camp, the kids have structured activities, art classes and English classes, and they play sports and go on little excursions. But what I particularly love about the philosophy of Canadian Island is the focus on the kitchen. The kids can take classes that teach them how to make some of the food they'll eat, including pasta made from scratch.

When I visit, my favorite time of day is dinnertime. Everyone eats together, and everyone gets the same food.

I know that some of the kids sometimes feel lonely being away from home. But sitting around the table together, eating the same thing, seems to ease all of that. The kids share the stories about where they're from, how they spent their day and what they're looking forward to doing tomorrow. It's one big, noisy, happy family.

ZIA MARIA'S TUSCAN SOUP

4 cups (1 L) cooked cannellini beans (page 10) or 2 cans (19 oz/540 mL) cannellini beans, rinsed and drained

2 cups (500 mL) passata

2 sprigs of fresh rosemary

Salt, QB

Freshly ground black pepper, QB

4 to 6 tbsp (60 to 90 mL) extra-virgin olive oil

The credit for this soup goes to my sister, Maria. She came up with this in a pinch one night for her son, Giovanni. He loved it so much that she serves it at her Canadian Island camp. Now she has my family hooked on it.

It's healthy and hearty. Surprisingly, even young kids who often don't like beans love this soup. The trick here is to run your beans through a food mill. The food mill not only purées the beans but also takes the skin off, giving the soup a silky texture.

Now when my kids see their Zia Maria, they ask for her creamy Canadian Island soup.

Pass the beans through a food mill into a pot. Discard the skins. Add the passata and 1 sprig of rosemary.

Place the pot on the stove over medium heat and bring the soup to a gentle simmer. Season with salt and pepper.

Pour the soup into individual bowls. Drizzle each with a tablespoon (15 mL) of olive oil and some rosemary needles.

SERVES 4 TO 6

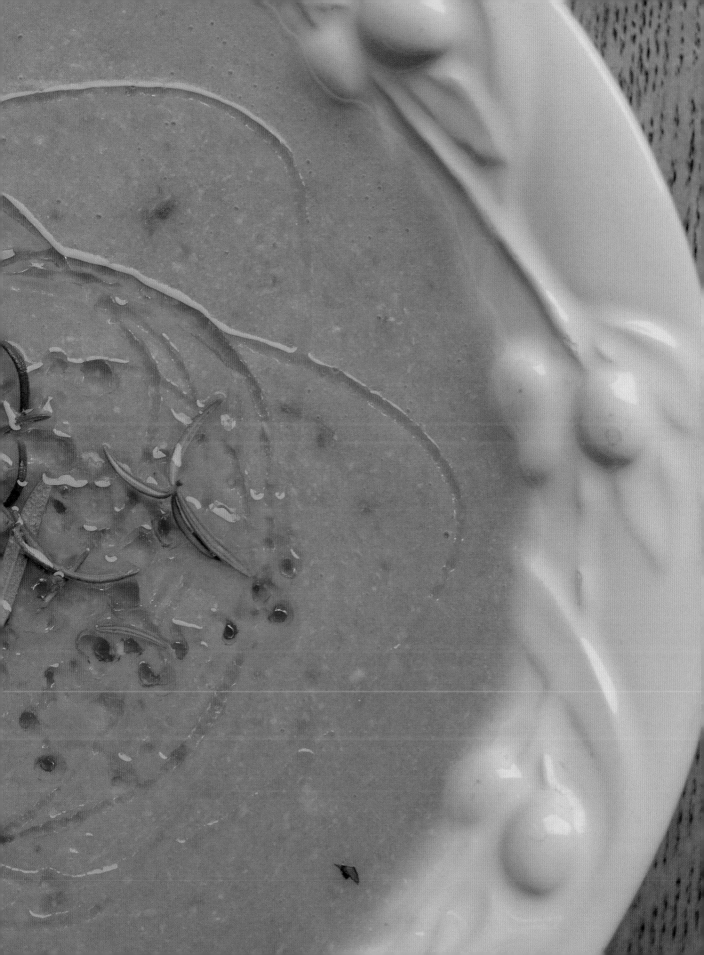

ZUCCHINI RISOTTO

Easy Vegetable Stock

2 carrots, roughly chopped

2 onions, quartered

2 stalks celery, roughly chopped

2 tomatoes, quartered

1 bunch fresh flat-leaf parsley

Zucchini Risotto

3 tbsp (45 mL) extra-virgin olive oil

2 small zucchini, cut into rounds

Salt, QB

Freshly ground black pepper, QB

3 tbsp (45 mL) extra-virgin olive oil

2 shallots, minced

2 cups (500 mL) arborio rice

Salt, QB

4 to 5 cups (1 to 1.25 L) warm Easy Vegetable Stock (recipe above)

1 glass dry white wine (optional)

2 tbsp (30 mL) butter

Freshly grated Parmigiano-Reggiano, QB

4 to 6 zucchini flowers, for garnish (optional)

Risotto is creamy and comforting—perfect for kids, so this is on my sister's menu. It's also a great way to get kids involved in cooking, since it requires a fair amount of stirring, which is easy for them to do, and they get to watch the dish develop right before their eyes.

My kids brag that they've been making risotto since they were three years old, when I used to let them stir while I was holding them. Now I just lay everything out and they actually make it themselves.

For this risotto you want to use vegetable stock. Chicken stock would overpower the zucchini. For the same reason, I like to use shallots instead of onion, but mild-flavored onions are fine if you don't have any shallots on hand.

Throw the vegetables into a big soup pot and fill it with water. Don't season it at all. You can take care of seasoning when you make the risotto. Bring it to a boil and then reduce the heat and let it simmer for 2 hours. At this point, strain it, discard the vegetables and put the clear stock back in the pot. Reduce the heat to low to keep the stock warm while you make your risotto.

Make sure your vegetable stock is heated up and ready to go.

Heat the olive oil in a frying pan over medium-high heat. Add the zucchini and a pinch of salt and pepper, and cook until the zucchini is soft. Set aside.

Follow the steps for Risotto Bianco (see page 29), using the next six ingredients. When the risotto is finished, take it off the heat.

Add the zucchini, butter and Parmigiano to your risotto and stir to combine. Serve. If you have some zucchini flowers, you can keep them whole as an edible garnish, or chop them up, and sprinkle them on top.

SERVES 4 TO 6

TUSCAN HERB MIX

Fresh rosemary

Fresh sage

Kosher or coarse sea salt

During their stay at camp, kids get to pick ingredients from the herb garden and then they go into the kitchen and make a classic Tuscan herb blend. Not only do they make the blend, but they get to take home a jar of it as a souvenir. And when they're home and it's used to make a meal, it's a little reminder of their time in Tuscany.

The herbs are blended with salt using a mezzaluna, which makes it relatively safe for kids to do. You do have to supervise, but the kids are so proud when they've helped in the kitchen.

Destem the rosemary by grabbing it from the top end and pulling straight against the growth. The needles should come off easily. Pull the sage leaves off their stems, as well.

Put what looks like equal amounts of rosemary needles and sage onto a cutting board, together with a good pinch of salt.

With a mezzaluna, rock back and forth over the herbs and salt until it's all pretty finely chopped and everything comes together. Scoop into a clean jar. This herb mix will keep in your cupboard for 3 to 4 months.

TUSCAN ROASTED POTATOES

White- or yellow-fleshed potatoes, peeled and roughly chopped, QB

Extra-virgin olive oil, QB

Tuscan Herb Mix (recipe above), QB

Preheat your oven to 350°F (180°C).

Place the potatoes on a rimmed baking sheet or in a roasting pan. Drizzle all over with olive oil. Sprinkle with the Tuscan Herb Mix and toss so that the potatoes are well coated.

Bake for 20 to 30 minutes or until the potatoes are crisp on the outside and fluffy on the inside.

ROAST BEEF

3 lb (1.5 kg) oven roast, like sirloin tip roast or round roast

1 head garlic, separated and all but 2 or 3 cloves peeled

10 sprigs of fresh rosemary, plus extra for searing beef

Kosher salt, QB

1/4 cup + 1/2 cup (60 + 125 mL) extra-virgin olive oil

1/4 cup (60 mL) Tuscan Herb Mix (page 258)

1 bottle (3 cups/750 mL) dry white wine

Soffritto (optional)

3 tbsp (45 mL) extra-virgin olive oil

1 onion, finely diced

2 carrots, finely diced

2 stalks celery, finely diced

Salt, QB

Freshly ground black pepper, QB

This is my mother's recipe. I like to use it because it's easy and makes a very flavorful roast beef.

Because a roast is a big, round hunk of meat that gets cooked whole, the meat itself can be a bit flavorless. But her recipe fixes the problem, with a technique that is easy and very low-tech. My only note is that it may look like you're using too much salt, garlic and rosemary. But don't worry. The flavors disperse through the thick part of the meat, giving the whole thing a wonderful flavor.

Preheat your oven to 400°F (200°C).

With the blade of a chef's knife, poke ten 3-inch-deep (7.5 cm) holes in the beef at regular intervals. (You can make the holes with the handle of a wooden spoon if you want; the goal is to make sizable holes that you can fill with aromatics.) Then, with your fingers, push a whole peeled garlic clove, a sprig of rosemary and as much salt as you can into each of the holes.

Once that's done, put the roast into a deep frying pan or Dutch oven. Rub the roast all over with 1/4 cup (60 mL) of olive oil, and then pour on the Tuscan Herb Mix and massage it in.

Put your pan on the stove and turn the heat up to high. Then pour in the remaining 1/2 cup (125 mL) of olive oil and start searing the roast on all sides. To the oil, add 2 or 3 unpeeled garlic cloves (leaving the skin on prevents the garlic from burning and becoming bitter) and some extra rosemary. Once the beef is seared on all sides and has a nice golden color, pour in the wine. Cook for about 5 to 8 minutes, basting the roast a few times.

Once the wine is reduced by half, carefully transfer the pan to the oven and let the roast finish cooking there, about 30 minutes for medium-rare.

Remove the pan from the oven and let the roast rest for 15 minutes before serving.

To serve your roast with a soffritto (optional): After the meat goes into the oven, heat about 3 tbsp (45 mL) of olive oil in a frying pan over medium heat. When the oil shimmers, add the onion, carrots and celery. Season with a little salt and pepper and cook until the vegetables are soft, about 15 minutes. When the roast is done, you can pour the soffritto into the pan with the juices and let it rest with the meat for 15 minutes before serving.

SERVES 6 TO 8

GIORGI GIRL'S CORNFLAKE COOKIES

2 eggs

2/3 cup (150 mL) granulated sugar

1 cup (250 mL) unsalted butter, room temperature

2 cups (500 mL) all-purpose flour

1/2 cup (125 mL) blanched almonds or pine nuts, roughly chopped

1/4 oz (7 g) instant dry yeast (1 small packet)

2 cups (500 mL) cornflake cereal

Icing sugar, for dusting

Strangely, I don't like to bake. Well, maybe not so strangely because I tend to be an improviser in the kitchen and that doesn't work for baking. But my daughter Giorgia loves these cookies, so I've started making them with her and her sister, Emma. I love watching them work in the kitchen. They get so focused, and they're so proud of their results. This is a simple and forgiving cookie recipe.

Preheat your oven to 350°F (180°C). Line a baking sheet with parchment paper.

In a mixing bowl, whisk together the eggs and sugar until the sugar is dissolved. Add the butter, 1/2 cup (125 mL) at a time, and whisk until smooth. Gradually sift the flour into the bowl, stirring as you go, and mix until combined. Add the chopped nuts and yeast and stir well.

Pour the cornflakes onto a plate.

Grab a bit of the dough (about the size of a golf ball) and roll it into a ball. Then roll the ball in the cornflakes until completely covered. Put the ball on the prepared baking sheet and lightly press down to slightly flatten it. Keep going until you've used up all the dough.

Bake for 10 minutes. When the cookies come out of the oven, dust them with icing sugar and let them sit until they're cool enough to handle (if you can resist them for that long). Store them in an airtight container for up to a week.

MAKES ABOUT 24 COOKIES

QUICK APRICOT JAM

2 lb (1 kg) fresh apricots

Brown sugar, QB

When apricots are in season I can't get enough of them. And lucky me, the grounds of Canadian Island have apricot trees. I love eating them right off the tree. But I also like to turn them into a quick jam.

This is not a conventional jam recipe—there is nothing added to preserve the fruit. You have to eat it within a week, but the trade-off is that it's incredibly easy to make.

I use apricots here, but you can use the same technique with any soft fruit.

Just one note: I use brown sugar when I make apricot jam. You can use granulated if you want. And I don't give you a quantity for the sugar for two reasons: (1) I find most jam too sweet, so my taste may not be your taste, and (2) the amount of sugar you add depends on the sweetness of your fruit. You really have to taste it as you go and add a little sugar at a time until you get it to where you want it.

Pull the apricots apart. Remove and discard the pits.

Put the fruit in a big pan over medium heat. Stirring occasionally so that it doesn't burn, cook the fruit until it starts to soften and fall apart, about 10 minutes. Sprinkle in the brown sugar. Cook for another 50 minutes, stirring occasionally and mashing up the bits of apricot to get a texture that you like. I like a thick purée, with a few chunks of fruit here and there.

Turn off the heat and let it cool. Put it in a jar and keep it in the fridge. It will keep for about a week.

MAKES ABOUT 4 CUPS (1 L)

DIANA
THE LAWYER

Diana Palomba is my Italian lawyer. Originally from Naples, schooled in England, she now lives in Florence, where she's raising two kids, her daughter, Clara, and her little boy, Rocco.

Beyond the fact that I think she's a great lawyer, I get a real kick out of the way she's a mix of old and new. There's something wonderful about being over at her place and talking to her about legal matters while she simultaneously makes a pasta from scratch, stops mid-thought to yell at one of her kids and then returns to whatever we're talking about, all the while kneading the dough. It's like watching her morph from a top-flight lawyer to an Italian *mamma* and back again.

Diana and I have been talking food almost since the day we first met. In the early days I'd call her for a quick five-minute legal chat and it would inevitably turn into a forty-five-minute exchange about what we were cooking. Afterward I would hang up and wonder just how much of that call I was paying for!

Diana learned to cook under the supervision of her Nonna Clara. According to Diana, her *nonna* could make anything in the kitchen and had such magic hands that even if she was out of yeast, the dough would obey her and rise. But my absolute favorite thing is this bit of wisdom from her Nonna Clara: "Above all in the kitchen, if you have passion and talent, you do not need to follow the recipes. They are only the base. You just have to let your *fantasia* go and inspire you."

I'm very fond of Diana. We've developed a friendship. And I have to say that she's given me a few recipes that are now part of my go-to repertoire.

I've always teased her that she'd be a better chef than a lawyer. Maybe it's a ploy to get my rates down a bit . . . But really, I don't want her to quit, because she's one of the best lawyers I know.

PASTA CON CREMA DI MELANZANE

1 lb (500 g) penne pasta

1/4 cup (60 mL) extra-virgin olive oil, plus more for drizzling

2 medium eggplants, unpeeled and cubed

Salt, QB

1/2 cup (125 mL) table (18%) or whipping (35%) cream (or QB)

1/2 cup (125 mL) freshly grated Parmigiano-Reggiano, plus more for finishing

1/4 cup (60 mL) pine nuts, toasted

10 cherry tomatoes, quartered

Fresh basil, QB

If you love eggplant—and I do love eggplant—this will become your new go-to dish. One weekend I had a business meeting with Diana at her house, and she invited me to stay for lunch. She wanted to make me one of her favorite eggplant dishes. Then she discovered she didn't have any passata, which is a key ingredient. She apologized profusely, but she needn't have. She improvised on the spot and what she made was mind-blowing. I've since had her dish with the passata and, honestly, I prefer it this way.

So, just like her *nonna* taught her, a little *fantasia* (inventiveness), is all you need to create something really spectacular.

Start making your sauce and pasta at the same time.

Put a large pot of water on to boil. When the water boils, salt it, drop in the penne and give it a quick stir.

Heat the olive oil in a large frying pan over high heat. When the oil shimmers, add the eggplant and season with some salt. Fry the eggplant, stirring occasionally, until soft and slightly golden.

Transfer the cooked eggplant to a blender. Add about 1/4 cup (60 mL) of the pasta cooking water (just scoop it out while the pasta is cooking) and the cream and Parmigiano. Blend until smooth. If there are some bits of skin, I personally don't mind that, but you can remove them if you want.

Pour the eggplant cream into the pan and warm it over medium heat.

Just before your penne is al dente, drain it, reserving about 1/2 cup (125 mL) of the pasta cooking water.

Add the cooked pasta to the eggplant cream along with a little bit more of the pasta cooking water (you may not need all of it; use just enough to loosen the sauce to desired consistency). Toss to combine, and finish cooking the pasta in the sauce for about a minute or so.

Divide the pasta among four serving plates and top each with the pine nuts, cherry tomatoes and a basil leaf. Finish with a drizzle of olive oil and a fresh grate of Parmigiano.

SERVES 4

FOCACCIA ROMANA

1 1/4 cups (300 mL) water, room temperature

1 tsp (5 mL) granulated sugar

1 packet (7g) instant dried yeast

3 1/3 cups (825 mL) all-purpose flour or Tipo 00 flour

1 tsp (5 mL) salt

2 tbsp (30 mL) extra-virgin olive oil, plus more for drizzling

Coarse sea salt, QB

The difference between focaccia and pizza is in the yeast. Focaccia uses more. As a result, the dough rises higher, resulting in a thicker bread. Diana says her Nonna Clara would make this daily for the family meal. Because it has to rise a few times, this is something Diana makes on weekends, for her kids.

You can make this dough using your hands or a stand mixer. It's up to you. If you are using a stand mixer, fit it with the dough hook.

Preheat your oven to 300°F (150°C). Once it reaches that temperature, turn it off.

In a small bowl, combine the water, sugar and yeast, mixing with your fingers until the sugar and yeast are dissolved. Let it sit for 5 minutes until the yeast starts to foam.

Pour the flour into a mixing bowl. Add the yeast mixture, a little at a time, mixing constantly with your fork. Add the salt and olive oil and continue mixing until the yeast mixture is completely incorporated.

Knead the dough until it is soft and smooth and shape it into a ball. Place the dough ball into a clean bowl and cover the bowl with a clean kitchen towel. Let it rest in the warmed oven for 2 hours, until doubled in size.

Sprinkle a bit of flour on a work surface, and turn the dough out. Knead it back and forth with the palm of your hand for a few minutes. Divide the dough into two halves and knead each half for a few more minutes.

Place the dough on a tray and cover with a damp kitchen towel. Set the tray aside for about 15 minutes so the dough can rest.

Generously grease two baking sheets with olive oil. Put each piece of dough on its own sheet. Using your hands, stretch the dough out so that it covers the entire sheet. Finish each with a generous drizzle of olive oil, and sprinkle with coarse salt. Let rest for 20 minutes at room temperature.

Preheat your oven to 425°F (220°C). When the loaves have rested and your oven is at temperature, bake for 15 minutes. You'll end up with Roman-style focaccia, which is crisp on the outside and soft and moist on the inside.

Top with your favorite salumi and wedges of fig.

MAKES 2 FOCACCIA

DANUBIO DI DIANA

2/3 cup (150 mL) milk

1 packet (7 g) instant dry yeast

3 1/3 cups (825 mL) bread flour or all-purpose flour

2 tbsp (30 mL) granulated sugar

2 tsp (10 mL) salt

1/4 cup (60 mL) extra-virgin olive oil

1 egg

Filling

3 oz (90 g) *prosciutto cotto* or cooked ham

8 oz (250 g) provola fresca or scamorza or caciocavallo

Egg Wash

1 egg

Splash of milk

Sesame seeds (optional)

Even though this looks fancy, it's actually about as old-school as it gets. It's a perfect way to use up odds and ends: leftover cheese, salami, different types of ham, whatever you have. As Diana says, it's what the *nonne* would do.

Danubio is a bunch of little buns, baked together. As they bake, they attach to each other, and when you serve it people just tear off their little portion. This makes it fun, especially for kids.

Because this dough calls for milk and sugar, it's slightly sweeter and softer than regular bread dough. The sweetness contrasts nicely with savory fillings like ham and cheese. You can also make a sweet version of *danubio* by stuffing the buns with a little chocolate.

In a saucepan, heat some milk until just slightly warmer than room temperature. Take it off the heat and add the yeast, gently stirring until dissolved. Let it rest for 5 minutes, until the yeast begins to foam.

Pour the flour, sugar and salt into a mixing bowl and add the yeast mixture. Then add the olive oil and 1 egg and, using a fork, mix until everything is incorporated.

Turn the dough out onto a lightly floured work surface. Knead until it comes together and forms a nice smooth, silky dough. Shape the dough into a ball and place it in a clean bowl. Cover the bowl with a clean kitchen towel and set aside in a warm place for about 2 hours, until the dough has doubled in size. Diana, like many Italian cooks I know, turns the light on in her oven and lets the dough do its thing in there.

While the dough is rising, line a 10-inch (25 cm) round ovenproof dish with parchment paper.

Now comes the fun part. Divide the dough into about thirty equal pieces. Press a few cubes of the meat and cheese into the center of each piece, seal the dough around the filling and roll into a ball. As you finish each ball, place it in the prepared dish in a single layer, starting along the outside rim. If they touch, that's okay. Keep going until the entire dish is filled.

To prepare the egg wash: In a bowl, whisk together the egg and milk. Brush the egg wash over the dough. Sprinkle with sesame seeds if using. Cover the pan with the kitchen towel and let it rest for an hour at room temperature.

Preheat your oven to 350°F (180°C).

Bake for about 30 to 35 minutes or until the top of the buns are golden. Remove from the oven and let the buns rest in the pan until they have come to room temperature.

MAKES ABOUT 30 BUNS

THE FISHERMEN OF ORBETELLO

O ver sixty years ago a group of fishermen in the Tuscan coastal town of Orbetello formed a co-op. Their goal was to protect their industry and preserve their jobs.

Today the Orbetello Pesca Lagunare is still going strong. The sons and grandsons of the founders are now running the businesses that grew from the original idea. They have a fishery, a smokehouse, a store where you can buy the fish and foods they produce (like bottarga) and a popular restaurant called I Pescatori. It's all housed in a renovated nineteenth-century stable that overlooks the very lagoon where they fish.

For the members of the co-op, being a fisherman is bigger than just taking in a good daily haul. They think of themselves as keepers of the lagoons. They've partnered with the World Wildlife Fund to protect their fishing area and the green space surrounding it. Their commitment to the environment extends to the ways in which they work. They still fish in the same ways as their grandfathers. They are mindful not to overfish. They throw back fish that are too small. In other words, this is not a greedy group of people. They think about the greater good and future generations.

I wanted to know what an average day was like for them, so I got up at 6 a.m. and went to the lagoon to fish with Sergio and Maurizio. It's an adventure I can best sum up by saying it was the first time I picked up a live eel.

We were back at shore around 11:30 a.m. Time for breakfast. The fishermen have a little grill set up not far from where they dock their boats. Using the seawater, we cleaned and washed some of the fish we'd just caught, then we grilled the fish with just a hit of sea salt. Sergio went into the little garden they have next to the lagoon to pick some fresh tomatoes. He sliced them up and served them drizzled in a little olive oil. They poured wine into small tumblers, nothing fancy. We all ate with our hands, standing around the grill in the fresh air, talking and laughing with the seagulls screaming overhead.

I spent the rest of the day exploring some of their other businesses.

What's cool about these fishermen is that they all do a bit of everything. They rotate jobs. They all take turns getting up in the morning and catching fish. Then they might work in the smokehouse for the rest of the day. Or they go to the restaurant. There's a schedule, but no hierarchy. You can be a waiter one day and a dishwasher or a line cook the next. By the end of my day I was charmed by their utter lack of ego, their strong sense of family and the joy that they take from their work.

Way past sundown, I wandered over to the restaurant. There were Sergio and Maurizio, my morning fishing buddies, on duty and still having fun.

The truth is you don't need a bond of blood to be a family. You can evolve into one through your business and a shared commitment to caring about where you live and who you are, just like the fishermen of Orbetello.

GRILLED FISH

When fish is served fresh straight from the sea, the lagoon, the lake, *leave it alone*. A little salt and then straight onto the hot grill. *Basta*. Stop. *Mangia. Buon appetito!*

BOTTARGA

5 oz (150 g) bottarga, thinly sliced

Freshly ground white pepper, QB

Extra-virgin olive oil, for drizzling

Crostini

Lemon wedges (optional)

Bottarga is salted, cured fish roe. Mullet roe, to be specific. It's sometimes called Mediterranean caviar. The fish eggs are salted, pressed together to form a block and then left to cure. It's one of the oldest processed foods in the world, dating back to ancient Egypt. But that's not going to help you in the kitchen, is it? I won't kid you. It's an acquired taste. And I'd like to describe it to you, but like caviar, it's hard to describe. It's salty and fishy, but in the best sense of the words. You don't cook bottarga. You can grate bottarga over pasta (I have a recipe for that later; see page 302) or you can serve it like sushi, as we do here. Nice slices, served in the simplest way possible. You can find it at specialty food stores and fish mongers.

Lay slices of bottarga on a serving platter. Season with white pepper and drizzle with olive oil. Serve with crostini and lemon wedges.

SERVES 2

SEA BREAM CARPACCIO

8 oz (250 g) skinless sea bream fillets

Juice of 1 lemon

Extra-virgin olive oil, for drizzling

Crostini

Thinly slice sea bream and arrange in a single layer on a serving platter. Squeeze lemon juice all over fish—the acid in the lemon will "cook" the raw fish. Let that sit for 10 to 15 minutes, until the flesh turns opaque. Drain any excess lemon juice. Drizzle with extra-virgin olive oil. Serve with crostini.

SERVES 2

TUNA AND CHICKPEA SALAD

2 cups (500 mL) cooked chickpeas (page 10) or 2 cans (19 oz/540 mL) chickpeas, rinsed and drained

2 stalks celery, chopped

1 pint (25 to 30) cherry tomatoes, quartered

7 oz (200 g) canned tuna (or palamita), in oil

Salt, QB

Freshly ground black pepper, QB

Dried chili flakes, QB

Extra-virgin olive oil, for drizzling

You know those late nights when you come home from work and you're tired and cranky and don't know what to make for dinner? This dish is perfect for those nights. It's packed with protein. And from having the aha! moment of remembering that you have the ingredients on hand to eating takes all of 10 minutes.

This is a very simple salad that you can make right in the serving bowl. Like so many quick Italian salads, it pays off with more flavor than you'd expect from such few ingredients. On the Tuscan coast, it's made with palamita, a relative of tuna that's abundant there, but it's just as tasty with tuna. If you have the time, I recommend cooking up some dried chickpeas. Of course, canned chickpeas will work, too. Just be sure to give them a good rinse under cold running water before adding them to the salad.

Put the chickpeas, celery, tomatoes and tuna in a big salad bowl and give it a good toss to combine. Add the seasonings and drizzle with olive oil to coat, or QB. Toss again and serve.

SERVES 4

SPAGHETTI WITH SMOKED EEL

1 lb (500 g) spaghettoni pasta (thick spaghetti)

7 oz (200 g) smoked marinated eels

1/4 cup (60 mL) + 2 tbsp (30 mL) extra-virgin olive oil

3 cloves garlic (unpeeled)

1 pint (25 to 30) cherry tomatoes, quartered

Eel is not a fish I've cozied up to over the years, but it is abundant in the lagoons of Orbetello. There, it's prepared using the Spanish method, by smoking the eel in a pepper and vinegar marinade. The flavor is fantastic and goes well with pasta.

Start making your sauce and pasta at the same time.

Put a large pot of water on to boil. The goal is to get the pasta to the al dente stage just as you're finishing the sauce, so you might want to salt the water and drop the pasta in while you're frying the eel.

Cut the eels into large chunks. Heat 1/4 cup (60 mL) olive oil in a frying pan over medium-high heat. Place the eel in the pan, skin-side down. When the eel pieces start to bend and fold up, in about 2 minutes, turn them over and cook them on the other side. Remove the eel. Using your fingers, pull off the skin and spine.

In the same frying pan, heat the remaining 2 tbsp (30 mL) of olive oil over medium-high heat. When the oil shimmers, add the garlic and tomatoes, and cook until the tomatoes soften. Add the fried eel and toss to combine. Cook for about 1 minute to let the flavors come together. Discard the garlic.

When the spaghettoni is moments away from being al dente, drain it, reserving 1/4 cup (60 mL) of the pasta cooking water.

Add the cooked pasta, along with the reserved cooking water, to the sauce and cook for about another minute. Serve immediately.

SERVES 4

SPAGHETTI ALLE VONGOLE CON BOTTARGA

2 lb (1 kg) clams (or QB)

1 lb (500 g) spaghetti pasta

1/4 cup (60 mL) extra-virgin olive oil, plus more for drizzling

3 cloves garlic, thinly sliced

1 tsp (5 mL) dried chili flakes

1 glass dry white wine

Salt, QB

1 bunch fresh flat-leaf parsley, chopped

3 tbsp (45 mL) grated bottarga, divided

The head chef at the restaurant is Davide. He started as a busboy, and by watching and learning, he worked his way up to head chef. Now Davide serves more than 40,000 plates a year! With his skill, he could go on to work at bigger or fancier restaurants if he wanted. When I asked him, he laughed a little self-consciously and then turned to the big open door and looked out at the sea. I get it. This is perfect. Why would he leave? Hanging out with Davide, I realized that in my next life I want to be a fisherman of Orbetello.

As a way of saying thank you, I asked Davide if I could stay and help make the staff meal, and this is what we made.

Rinse your clams well under cold running water. Discard any that are open.

Start making your sauce and pasta at the same time.

Put a large pot of water on to boil. When the water boils, salt it, drop in the pasta and give it a gentle stir.

In a frying pan that has a lid and is big enough to hold the clams, heat the olive oil over medium heat. When the oil shimmers, add the garlic and chili flakes, and cook for 30 seconds. Then add all of the clams. Pick up your wine, take a sip and throw the rest in with the clams. Increase the heat to high, cover the pan with the lid and gently shake the pan. Cook until all the clams open, 3 to 5 minutes.

Discard any clams that haven't opened. Reduce the heat to low. Add a little salt and the parsley, and toss.

Take half of the clams out of the shells, discarding the empty shells and returning the clam meat to the pan.

When your pasta is about 30 seconds away from being al dente, drain it, reserving about 1/2 cup (125 mL) of the pasta cooking water.

Add the cooked pasta, along with some of the reserved pasta cooking water, to the clams. Use just enough reserved cooking water to loosen the sauce. Toss it together for 30 seconds to combine. The pasta will finish cooking in the sauce and release starches to give the sauce some body. Remove the pot from the heat and add 2 tbsp (30 mL) of the bottarga. Give the pan another toss.

Divide the pasta and the clams evenly among the serving bowls. Drizzle with olive oil and sprinkle a bit of bottarga over each dish.

Serve immediately.

SERVES 4

THE
MATTIUCCI
BROTHERS

Early one morning I was walking down the street in Naples when I noticed a *pescheria* (fish shop) called Pescheria Mattiucci. Now, there's nothing unusual about a fish shop that's open in the early morning, but this little shop was quite eye-catching. It had the traditional blue-and-white tile decorations that you see in a lot of fish shops in this part of Italy, but it looked a little bit more like a boutique.

When I was headed home that evening, walking down the same street, I could hear that the little shop was open even before I got to it. This intrigued me. By that time of day most fish shops would have sold out and closed up. When I got there, I saw that the little *pescheria* had turned into a *crudo* bar (*crudo* means "raw"). People were standing around with little plates of food and glasses of wine. So I went in.

Pescheria Mattiucci was established by the eldest Mattiucci brother, Luigi. And then his younger brothers, Gennaro and Francesco, joined him. They come from a family of fishermen who set their business up in the 1890s. Their history is reflected in the century-old family photos that decorate the *pescheria*.

Eating raw fish isn't new to Southern Italy, where it is very hot. Back in the days when there were no refrigerators, the fishermen would make *crudo* dishes when they had leftovers from the day's catch that they couldn't store. They'd cut up the fish, squeeze a bit of lemon and maybe sprinkle some sea salt over it, and that would be their meal.

Now, I've eaten raw fish in Italy before, but the Mattiuccis are at another level altogether. They serve their *crudo* with berries, fruit, raw vegetables and herbs—inventive combinations. Even the way they serve it is exciting. The plates all look like edible art.

Pescheria Mattiucci is an intimate space. When I was there, Gennaro was making the *crudo*. When I reacted with obvious excitement, *he* got excited and began making me some of the house specialties—combinations that I had never considered before. Honestly, it was one of the most inspiring evenings that my palate had had in a while. Like so many of their generation, the Mattiucci brothers have taken a job that would normally be thought of as a humble trade and put a glamorous spin on it.

Traditionally, fishermen and fishmongers would sell their catch at the dock, where they didn't have to pay rent and could find cheap labor. And at one time the Mattiuccis had a fish stall in the main market. But the Mattiucci brothers' passion and culinary talent has moved the business into new areas. Now their little *pescheria* is in the upscale Chiaia area of Naples. They are still proudly honoring the family tradition, but pushing it forward so that it speaks to a new generation.

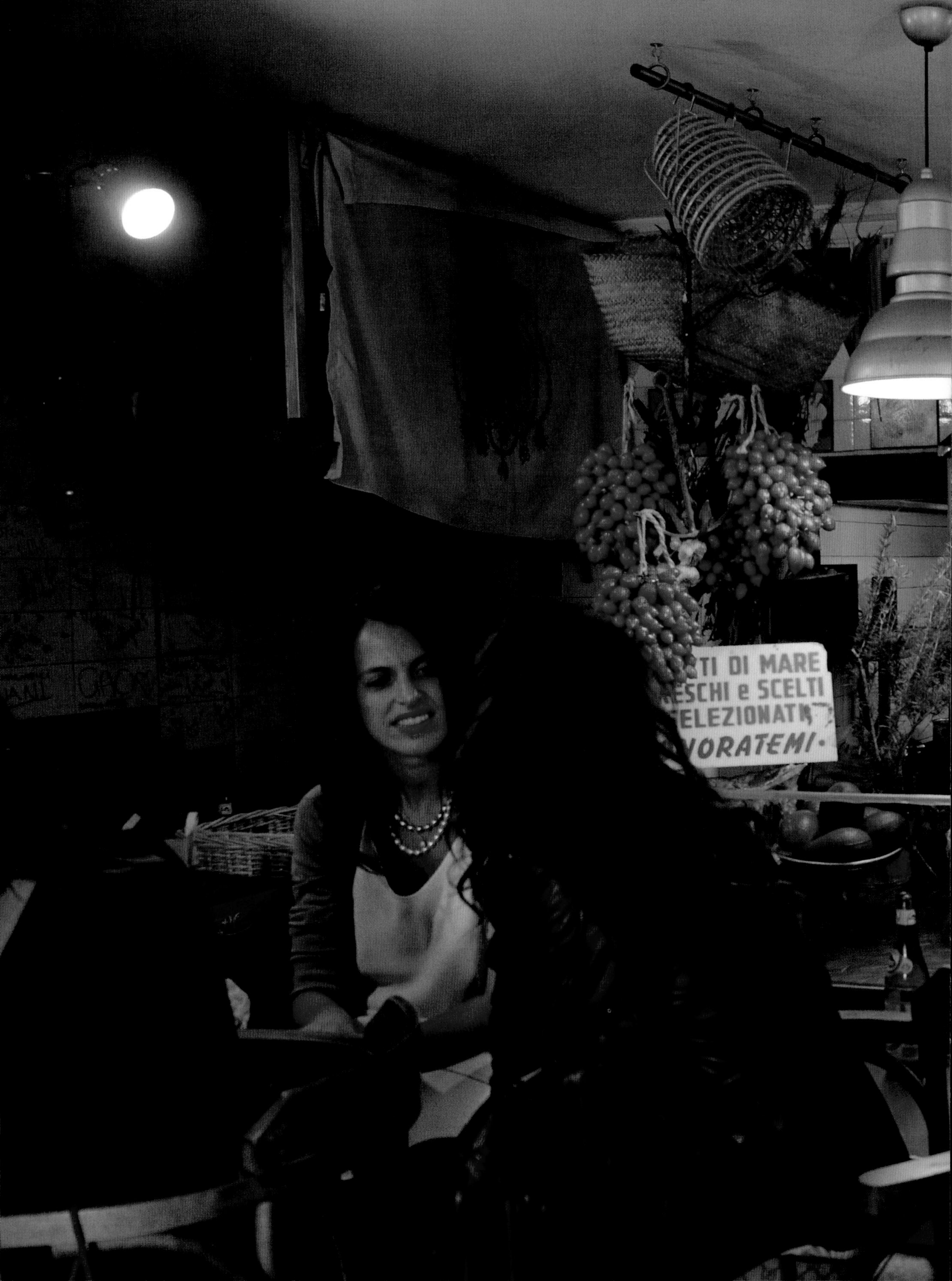
TI DI MARE
ESCHI e SCELTI
ELEZIONATI
ORATEMI.

THE BELLAVISTA IN IMPRUNETA

In the mid-1400s, when the great Filippo Brunelleschi was building the dome for the Cattedrale Santa Maria del Fiore, better known as the Duomo di Firenze, he insisted that all the tiles for its terra-cotta dome come from the town of Impruneta. And he used to go there himself on a regular basis to check the tiles. Hundreds of years later, that terra-cotta dome, which is the largest in the world, is still a marvel of Renaissance workmanship and a testament to the resilience of those tiles.

Impruneta is a little village about twenty minutes outside of Florence, and it's still famous for its terra-cotta. But that isn't the only tradition that has come down the ages from this little town. It's also famous for a peppery beef stew called *peposo*.

The Bellavista Hotel in Impruneta makes an award-winning *peposo* that has been named "the most authentic in Italy." So of course I had to try it.

The hotel is located in the center of Impruneta, on the town's main square. The business is owned by Beppe and Roberta Beccuci, who run it with their three children, Matteo, Tomasso and Martina. Beppe is a bit of a prankster, as well as a high-energy showman, but when it comes to making his Tuscan *peposo*, the show is over. Beppe is all business. He doesn't play games with his *peposo*, and it is fantastic.

I watched him make this dish the same way his family has made it for several generations. We then ate together, with his two sons, on the restaurant terrace overlooking the city's piazza and those ageless terra-cotta tiles.

TUSCAN PEPOSO

4 1/2 lb (2.25 kg) stewing beef, including some gristle

1 head garlic, cloves peeled and left whole

1/2 cup (125 mL) freshly ground black pepper (or QB)

4 cups (1 L) thick tomato sauce

Coarse sea salt, QB

1 bottle (3 cups/750 mL) Chianti or similar dry red wine

The people of Impruneta may have made great tiles, but they weren't rich. Out of necessity, they often had to buy cuts of meat that were starting to go off and were sold at a cheaper price. The other things that were plentiful and cheap were red wine and pepper. And that is the basis of Tuscan Peposo.

The wine and pepper break down the meat, as does the long, slow simmering time. The final dish is tender and delicious. My bet is that Brunelleschi didn't make the trip to Impruneta just to see tiles. As with any stew, this gets better with time, so you can definitely make it in advance. It will keep in your fridge for about 5 days.

Put all the ingredients in a large pot. Bring to a boil, reduce the heat to a simmer, put the lid on and let it cook for 4 to 5 hours. Turn off the burner and let the pot rest for an hour with the lid on. Serve with Tuscan bread.

SERVES 8 TO 10

SIMONE FROM CASENTINO

Man, I feel for Simone. Not the grown-up guy who makes some of the most delicious prosciutto on the face of the planet, but his childhood self. As a kid, before Simone was allowed to go play soccer, he had to do his chores. And on a family pig farm, that meant helping his father clean up the pens. And then he'd race off to play soccer. The kids used to call him *puzza piede* (stinky feet). It bothered him a lot back then. Oh, the pain!

Today, though, it's all good. Those same kids—now grown up, of course—come into his shop to buy his prosciutto. (I wonder if he gives them deals or charges them a bit more?)

I love prosciutto! But not all is created equal. It can be too tough, too salty, even too bland. And then there's Simone's: His prosciutto has more fat than other types, which gives it incredible flavor, and it almost melts in your mouth. Simone has won national awards for it in Italy. The world knows Prosciutto di Parma. But Simone's Prosciutto di Casentino is next-level.

Simone is Simone Fracasse, who is the latest in his family to run the butcher shop Antica Macelleria Fracasse. It was founded by his grandfather, and Simone, taking up the business with loving care, has kept it a veritable wonderland for food lovers.

Like many of the best producers in the country, Simone maintains control of his final product, which starts by raising his own pigs. Every step in the life of his animals is important to him. He feeds his pigs a special diet of legumes and grains that he grinds into a powder so it's easy for them to digest. These are free-range pigs that also roam and forage. In their own way, his pigs are living *la dolce vita.*

Maybe it's unusual to think of a butcher as someone who cares about the quality of life for animals he'll eventually kill, but this is something that is true of all the best butchers I've met. Their work reflects a tremendous respect for the animals.

In case you've never heard of this little jewel of an area, Casentino is about a forty-five-minute drive from Florence. For my time and money—and serious cravings for prosciutto—it's well worth the drive there.

SIMONE'S PROSCIUTTO

Making great prosciutto takes time, patience and, some would say, happy pigs.

Simone's pigs are happy pigs. Simone feeds them well, and they're not penned up all day. They get to wander and forage to their hearts' content. This is important and special because it shows respect for the lives of the animals. And when their time comes, this good and happy life contributes to the flavor of the meat. The pigs have a large amount of fat, which gives the prosciutto a more delicate, almost creamy flavor.

Prosciutto is made from the hind leg of the pig. Simone walked me through the process. The meat is salted and left to hang for twenty to thirty days. Then the salt is washed off and the meat is left for another sixty days. At that point the first fatty layer is cut off. Simone then coats the meat in a mixture of lard, salt and flour that protects the prosciutto from drying out. The meat is then left to cure for two years.

In the case of an artisan like Simone, the reward is seeing the pleasure people take from his product. His prosciutto is beautiful eaten on its own with a piece of bread and a glass of wine. It's often served as part of an antipasto platter.

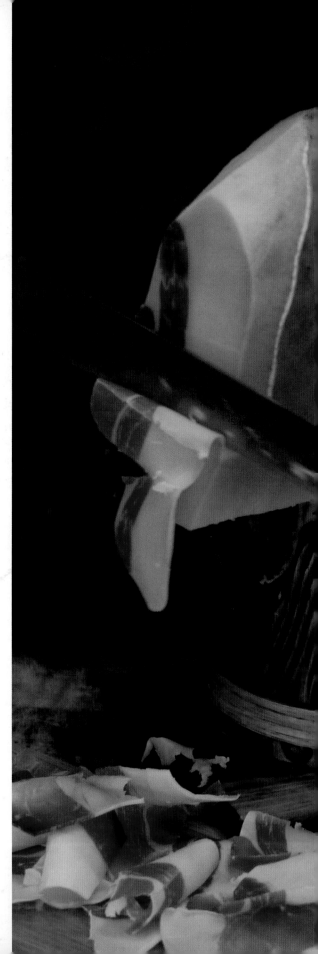

PROSCUITTO E MELONE

In the summer, when melons are ripe and fresh, this is a very common starter in Italy. It's all about the contrast of the sweet cantaloupe and the tender, slightly salty, prosciutto.

SIMONE'S BEEF RAGÙ TWO WAYS

Beef Ragù in White Wine Sauce

1/4 cup + 1 tbsp (60 + 15 mL) extra-virgin olive oil

1 medium onion, chopped

1 large carrot, chopped

1 stalk celery, chopped

Salt, QB

1 cup (250 mL) dry white wine

1 lb (500 g) ground beef

2 cups (500 mL) beef stock

1 lb (500 g) tagliatelle pasta

Beef Ragù in Red Wine Sauce

1/4 cup + 1 tbsp (60 + 15 mL) extra-virgin olive oil

1 large onion, chopped

1 large carrot, chopped

1 stalk celery, chopped

Salt, QB

1 cup (250 mL) red wine

1 lb (500 g) ground beef

1 tbsp (15 mL) tomato paste

1 cup (250 mL) tomato purée

1 cup (250 mL) beef stock

1 lb (500 g) pappardelle pasta

Freshly grated Parmigiano-Reggiano, QB

Extra-virgin olive oil, for drizzling

Like most butchers, Simone isn't just a guy who sells meat. He can hold his own in the kitchen. At his butcher shop he sells an assortment of ragùs, including these two, which are made from his family's recipes.

Start by making a soffritto: Heat 1/4 cup (60 mL) of olive oil in a large pot over medium-high heat. When the oil shimmers, add the onion, carrot, celery and a good pinch of salt and sauté until the vegetables are softened. Add half of your wine—white wine for the white ragù, red wine for the red ragù—and let it reduce for a few minutes.

Now, Simone's family removes the soffritto from the pot and sets it aside, but you can leave the soffritto in there if you want. Both methods work.

Reduce the heat to medium and add the remaining tablespoon (15 mL) of olive oil to the pot. Then add the ground beef and a pinch of salt, and cook until the meat is browned. Stir in the other half of your wine and cook for another 2 or 3 minutes, until it's almost completely evaporated.

For the white ragù: If you've removed the soffritto, add it to the pot. Pour in the beef stock and stir. Cover the pot with a lid, reduce the heat to low and let it simmer for 2 hours, stirring occasionally.

For the red ragù: If you've removed the soffritto, add it to the pot. Add the tomato paste and tomato purée. Pour in the beef stock and stir. Cover the pot with a lid, reduce the heat to low and let it simmer for 2 hours, stirring occasionally.

Just before the ragù is ready, cook your pasta. Put a large pot of water on to boil. When the water boils, salt it, drop in the pasta, give it a gentle stir and cook until al dente.

Drain it, reserving about 1/2 cup (125 mL) of the pasta cooking water.

Add the cooked pasta to the sauce, along with a bit of the reserved pasta cooking water, and let that cook together for a minute.

Remove the pan from the heat. Sprinkle the pasta with the Parmigiano and drizzle with olive oil.

Serve immediately.

SERVES 4 TO 6

KATIA'S TORTELLI

Filling

7 oz (200 g) pancetta, finely diced

1 tbsp (15 mL) extra-virgin olive oil

5 potatoes, peeled, boiled and cooled

1 cup (250 mL) passata

1 cup (250 mL) freshly grated Parmigiano-Reggiano

1 egg

1 tsp (5 mL) ground nutmeg

Salt, QB

Freshly ground black pepper, QB

Tortelli

1 batch Fresh Pasta Dough (page 13)

Sauce

Handful of freshly grated Parmigiano-Reggiano

Good-quality extra-virgin olive oil, QB

Simone's wife, Katia, is a great cook in her own right. At a meal with friends and family, she whipped these up on the spot. This recipe may look intimidating, but trust me, it's not. Give it a try.

To make the filling: In a frying pan, sauté the pancetta in the olive oil until the pancetta is lightly golden. Set aside to cool to room temperature.

Run the potatoes through a ricer into a bowl, or mash with a fork. Add the cooked pancetta and the passata, Parmigiano, egg, nutmeg and salt and pepper. Stir together until it's nice and creamy, and everything is evenly distributed. Taste for seasonings and adjust accordingly. Let it rest for half an hour.

To make the tortelli: Divide the dough into three equal portions. Working with one portion at a time, roll the pasta into sheets—either with a pasta machine (see Using a Pasta Machine, page 16) or by rolling pin on a lightly floured work surface. You don't want this dough to be too thin because the filling is heavy, so make it just a bit thicker than if it were spaghetti. Continue until you use up all your dough.

Lightly dust your work surface with flour so the pasta doesn't stick, and lay 1 sheet down lengthwise. Starting at one end, working along the length of the sheet, place a tablespoon (15 mL) of the filling about 2 inches (5 cm) from the top edge of the pasta sheet. Put another tablespoon (15 mL) of filling about 1 inch (2.5 cm) from the first. Continue until you have a row of the filling across the top of the pasta sheet.

Fold the bottom of the pasta sheet over the filling. Press the edge to seal. Press down between mounds to make the tortelli. Cut into individual pieces with a pasta wheel or a small sharp knife.

To cook the tortelli: Put a large pot of water on to boil. When the water boils, salt it, and drop in the pasta. Fresh pasta cooks quickly, in 2 to 3 minutes, so when the tortelli rise to the surface, they're done.

To make the sauce: When the filling is this good, you just need a very basic sauce. Using a slotted spoon, transfer the cooked tortelli to a frying pan with about a 1/4 cup (60 mL) of the pasta cooking water, a handful of Parmigiano and a good drizzle of extra-virgin olive oil. Toss gently to combine.

Serve immediately.

SERVES 4 TO 6

MY BUDDY
DARIO CECCHINI

ANTICA MACELLERIA

Dario Cecchini has a butcher shop and restaurants in Panzano in Chianti. He just might be the most famous butcher in the world. For certain he's the most famous one in Italy and in Europe.

His passion for quality is unrelenting, and his roster of clients includes rock stars and royalty.

Dario is an eighth-generation butcher who can list the names of all the Cecchinis who came before him. His eyes well up when he talks about cooking with his mother and grandmother. His heritage and family is important to him, and he wants to make his family proud.

A deeply philosophical man, Dario has a passion for animals. He believes that the exchange of an animal's life for our survival and enjoyment is a heavy responsibility that has to be respected, and he does that in several ways. When you kill an animal for food, you must honor its life and its sacrifice by eating every bit of it. Dario refuses to sell or serve veal. He believes that before the animal is slaughtered it must be treated well and live a long life.

Dario has his own herd of Chianina cows. They're an ancient breed, native to Tuscany. These white cows are huge, the size of oxen. At one time they would have been draft animals on the farm and considered part of the family. At the end of a cow's life it would be slaughtered for meat. The loss of an animal would be a heavy burden on the family, so they would use every part of the animal as a sign of respect. But now it's easy to go to a butcher shop and order the best cut of meat, then go home, slap on some salt and pepper, grill it to a nice medium-rare and feel good about life.

Dario is on a mission. He wants to teach us that there is beauty in the cuts we generally think of as discards. And so the last time I was with Dario he took me to a new place when it came to cooking beef. This is the ultimate in the kind of cooking that inspires me—*cucina povera,* peasant cooking, where nothing came easy, so nothing went to waste.

TENERUMI IN INSALATA

5 lb (2.5 kg) mixed beef cuts, including tendons, bones and cartilage

1 red onion, sliced, plus extra julienned for garnish, QB

2 carrots, roughly chopped, plus extra julienned for garnish, QB

2 stalks celery, roughly chopped, plus extra julienned for garnish, QB

Good-quality extra-virgin olive oil for drizzling

Red wine vinegar for drizzling

Freshly cracked black pepper, to finish

If I were to say to you, "Hey, come over. I'm going to make a great meal of cartilage and tendons," I could understand why your first impulse might be to politely say no. But hear me out: I think the issue is that most of us have grown up thinking that these cuts are for the garbage, and that there's something wrong with eating them. The truth is that if you set that conditioning aside, these are just other cuts of meat capable of being the basis of great meals. And with the right cooking technique, they're as tasty anything else.

So this uses bits of meat that might be unfamiliar to you, but beyond that it's very simple. It's a basic *bollito*, a technique people have been using for generations to soften tough cuts of meat. You'll be left with a delicious broth and tender, luscious meat to use in the following two recipes (below and page 341).

When I was there, Dario served us a little bit of the broth in teacups, which was really charming, and also really comforting to have alongside the meal.

For the tenerumi: Rinse the meat, bones, tendons and cartilage under cool running water and set aside.

Fill a big pot with cold water and put it over high heat. Add the onion, carrots and celery, and bring to a boil. When it's boiling, add the meat, bones, tendons and cartilage and cook for 5 minutes. It's kind of like searing the meat in boiling water. Reduce the heat to medium and let it simmer, periodically skimming off any foam or scum that rises to the top.

After 3 1/2 hours, the meat will be fall-off-the-bone tender, and the cartilage and tendons will be soft. With a slotted spoon, transfer the meat to a bowl and set aside to cool.

Strain the broth into a clean pot through a fine-mesh sieve to remove all the bits. Discard the vegetables and the bones. Keep everything else. Now you have broth, and enough meat to make the next two recipes.

For the insalata: This is a nicely balanced dish. The crisp raw vegetables are a perfect contrast to the soft, flavorful meat. It's all QB. You'll need thinly sliced red onion, julienned carrot and celery.

When the meat is cool enough to handle, take about 2 pounds (1 kg), chop it all—meat, tendons, everything—into small pieces, and place on a serving platter. Sprinkle with salt. Top with julienned carrots, celery and onion. Drizzle with good extra-virgin olive oil and red wine vinegar, sprinkle with freshly cracked black pepper and serve.

SERVES 6 TO 8

LA FAMIGLIA DELL'ANTICA
MACELLERIA CECCHINI

"RIDOTTA INVALIDA
PREFERI LA MORTE"
IN MEMORIA
DELLA
BISTECCA
ALLA FIORENTINA
SCOMPARSA PREMATURAMENTE
IL 31 MARZO 2001

LE MIE PREGHIERE ALFIN FURONO ACCOLTE
TORNA LA FIOR... LE BEN CI AZZECCA
INVALIDA MORÌ
VISSE DUE VOLT...
E INFATTI IL NO... IO COM'E:
BISTECCA!

ALBERTO SEVERI PER DARIO ...ECCHINI IL 1 GENNAIO 2006

LA FRANCESINA

1 can (28 oz/796 mL) peeled plum tomatoes, with juices

1/2 cup (125 mL) extra-virgin olive oil, divided

2 large red onions, thinly sliced

Salt, QB

Freshly ground black pepper, QB

2 lb (1 kg) cooked beef, tendons and cartilage (page 337)

This is another dish you can make with the meat from your *tenerumi* (page 337). It's a supremely comforting dish and may be my favorite of all that I had at Dario's. It's like a thick tomato beef stew with caramelized onions. I absolutely love it.

Pour the tomatoes in a bowl and use your hands to crush them to your desired consistency. Heat 1/4 cup (60 mL) of the olive oil in a large frying pan over medium heat. When the oil shimmers, add half of the onion and cook, slowly browning it, until it turns golden and begins to caramelize, about 15 minutes.

Then add the peeled plum tomatoes and season with salt and pepper. Cook for few minutes, until the sauce begins to reduce and thicken up.

Then in go the beef, tendons and cartilage. Let that cook for another 10 minutes. Turn off the heat and let it rest for a few minutes while you prepare the remaining onion.

In a separate frying pan, heat the remaining 1/4 cup (60 mL) olive oil over medium heat. Add the remaining onion, with a little bit of salt, and sauté until the onion is slightly softened but still has a little crunch. Add it to the *francesina* and serve immediately.

SERVES 6 TO 8

BEEF TARTARE WITH ROSEMARY

1 lb (500 g) beef tenderloin or sirloin, minced

1 clove garlic, minced

1 tsp (5 mL) sweet paprika

1 tbsp (15 mL) fresh flat-leaf parsley, finely chopped

1 tsp (5 mL) kosher salt

1 tsp (5 mL) freshly cracked black pepper

12 sprigs fresh rosemary

1/2 cup (125 mL) extra-virgin olive oil for frying, plus more for drizzling

One of the advantages of getting to know a good butcher is that you can buy the absolute freshest organic beef. Let them know you're making tartare, and buy it as close to the time you're going to serve it as possible.

This is one of Dario's signature appetizers that he shared with me. It's a mash-up of some of my favorite foods: moist and flavorful beef tartare and fried meatballs. Frying the tartare slightly gives the balls contrasting textures and flavors.

Dario uses the meat from the leg, the round, the shank and the brisket. This is not a usual maneuver for tartare because the meat, although lean, is tougher. Dario puts his meat through a tenderizing machine a few times, and that makes it soft and delicious. If you're not in Panzano in Chianti ask your butcher what they'd recommend so that you get the best and freshest product. They can hand-mince it and tenderize it for you, or you can finely chop it yourself and run it through a grinder a few times.

Put the meat in a mixing bowl and add the garlic, paprika, parsley, salt and pepper.

Roll the mixture into 12 golf-size balls. Insert a sprig of rosemary into each ball so that the top is sticking out.

Heat the olive oil in a frying pan over high heat. When the oil shimmers, carefully place each ball into the pan and cook until the bottom is golden brown and develops a nice crust. The top will still be raw, and that's what you're looking for.

Then remove the balls from the pan and put them on a plate lined with paper towels to absorb any excess oil.

Serve the tartare, as Dario does, with a good drizzle of excellent Tuscan extra-virgin olive oil.

MAKES 12 BALLS

CANTALOUPE AND RED ONION SALAD

1 ripe cantaloupe, rind removed, seeded and cubed

1/2 red onion, diced

Salt, QB

Juice of 1 orange

1/4 cup (60 mL) extra-virgin olive oil

I made the next two salads for Dario to accompany our big meat feast. These salads are easy, with only a few ingredients, but don't take them for granted. They're a surprising combination of contrasting flavors, sweetness and texture. Individually, the ingredients are delicious. Together, they excite the palate.

Place the cantaloupe and onion in a bowl. Add some salt. Squeeze the orange over them. And then add the olive oil. Mix carefully, and you're done!

SERVES 6 TO 8

ORANGE, FENNEL AND ONION SALAD

2 oranges + 1/2 an orange for juicing

1 bulb fennel, thinly sliced

1/2 red onion, thinly sliced

Salt, QB

1/4 cup (60 mL) good-quality extra-virgin olive oil

I love mixing fruit and vegetables in a salad. It's partly the texture—the crunchy versus the soft—and partly the flavor contrast of sweet orange, licoricey fennel and spicy onion. It's light and crisp and refreshing. One note: When you're breaking up your oranges, make sure to remove all of the bitter pith.

Peel and segment 2 oranges.

Place the orange segments, fennel and onion in a large bowl. Squeeze the juice of half an orange over everything. Add some salt and the extra-virgin olive oil. Gently toss so you don't break the orange segments.

Unlike a green salad, which should be served immediately after dressing, this one needs to sit for 15 minutes before serving.

SERVES 6 TO 8

PEACHES AND WINE

Peaches and wine in Panzano in Chianti is like the perfect marriage. To experience it yourself, slice some peaches and put them in a pitcher. Pour a simple table wine, like a Chianti, over them and let them sit for about half an hour. Take the peaches out, and serve the wine with dinner, and your peaches for dessert.

MY AMALFI FAMILY

Vincenzo Palumbo is a hotelier with three family-run hotels in the small town of Ravello, perched above the Amalfi Coast. He's a quiet, elegant and reserved man who loves the hospitality business and loves going the extra mile for his guests.

I met Vincenzo for the first time when I was working in Amalfi in 1999. The following year my wife, Nina, and I went back to Italy and stopped in Ravello for what was supposed to be a few days, just to say hi. But the day before we were supposed to leave, Vincenzo, who is known in the area as Il Professore, said, "Why don't you stay a few more days?" So we did. And then a few days later he made the same suggestion, and we said, "Sure!" We ended up spending our entire three-week vacation there, hanging around with the Prof, his family and his extended family, which included a wild Neapolitan singer and storyteller named Eddie Oliva.

For the entire three weeks, Nina and I never had a meal where it was just the two of us. We'd all sit down to dinner together and have these wide-ranging discussions that would go on for hours, helped along by the Prof's homemade *limoncello.* Then Eddie would pull out his guitar and start making up songs about whatever we had been discussing that would make us laugh until we cried.

I think that this isn't a relationship that grew into family. It felt like family from the moment Vincenzo and I sat down together for the first time.

Now that Nina and I have kids, we take them to Amalfi, where the Prof is now known as Zio Vincenzo.

VINCENZO'S CAPONATA MARE E MONTI

12 fresh shrimp, peeled and deveined

2 tbsp (30 mL) + 1/2 cup (125 mL) extra-virgin olive oil, plus more for drizzling

Zest and juice of 1 orange

4 *friselle* halves or 4 thick slices of Italian bread, double baked

10 cherry tomatoes, quartered

2 large balls mozzarella, cubed

Salt, QB

Freshly ground black pepper, QB

6 fresh basil leaves, torn

This is a Neapolitan caponata, not to be confused with Sicilian caponata, which is a stewed eggplant dish. The Neapolitan version uses *friselle,* a dried bagel-shaped bread. It's as dry as a cracker, so it's usually dipped quickly in water before it's used.

This caponata is a classic in the area around Naples. It's a delicious and light dish that you can prepare in moments, so it's perfect for summer.

At its most basic, caponata is a simple tomato-mozzarella-basil salad. But Vincenzo always fancies it up for me by adding in freshly marinated shrimp. When you make this dish, make sure your shrimp are absolutely fresh.

In a bowl, put the shrimp, 2 tbsp (30 mL) of the olive oil and orange zest. Toss to combine and set aside for 10 minutes to marinate.

Revive your *friselle* by giving them a very quick dip in a bowl of water. Don't soak them too much. You still want them to have crunch, and you don't want a *pappa* or mushy mess. Break them up into large croutons and put them into a large mixing bowl. Add the tomatoes and mozzarella, and 1/2 cup (125 mL) of the olive oil. Season with salt and pepper and give it a good mix. Divide it equally among four plates.

When your shrimp have finished marinating (if the shrimp are very fresh, don't worry if they're semi-raw—I like them that way), remove them from the marinade and top each plate with an equal amount of shrimp, some basil and a drizzle of olive oil.

SERVES 4

ORANGE CHICKEN WITH ALMONDS

4 boneless, skinless chicken breasts, pounded thin

Salt, QB

Freshly ground black pepper, QB

All-purpose flour, for dredging

3 tbsp (45 mL) extra-virgin olive oil

2 tbsp (30 mL) butter, divided

Juice of 2 oranges

Zest of 1 orange

1/2 cup (125 mL) blanched almonds, toasted

Fresh basil leaves, shredded or torn

Amalfi is known for its incredible lemons, but on our last vacation there my son, Dante (who was three at the time), wanted orange juice with his all of his meals. I'd always say no because no self-respecting Italian father would allow his son to have orange juice with pasta! So one night to make Little D happy, Zio Vincenzo had his chefs at Hotel Villa Maria whip up this dish, which is now a family staple.

Season the chicken breasts with salt and pepper. Place the flour on a plate and dredge the chicken on both sides, shaking off any excess flour.

Heat the olive oil and one tablespoon (15 mL) of the butter in a frying pan over medium heat. When the butter has melted, add the chicken breasts and cook for 4 to 5 minutes per side, until the juices run clear. Transfer the chicken to a serving plate.

To the same frying pan, add the orange juice and half of the zest. Dredge the remaining tablespoon (15 mL) of butter in the flour and add that to the pan to thicken up the sauce. Season with salt and pepper. Increase the heat to high and cook until the sauce has reduced by half. Then toss in the almonds and stir well. Turn off the heat and let it sit for about 20 seconds.

Pour the almonds and the orange sauce over the chicken. Top with the rest of the orange zest and the basil.

SERVES 4

CARLA'S BAKED CROSTATA DI RICOTTA

Pastry

3 1/3 cups (825 mL) Tipo 00 flour or all-purpose flour

1 tbsp (15 mL) baking powder

7 oz (200 g) granulated sugar

7 oz (200 g) unsalted butter, cold

3 egg yolks

1 egg

Zest of 1 lemon

Filling

3 egg whites

1 1/4 cups (300 mL) granulated sugar

1 1/2 lb (750 g) ricotta

Zest of 1 lemon

Icing sugar, for dusting

Carla is Vincenzo's wife. Her grandfather was a baker, so being good with pastry and sweets runs in the family.

When Carla's grandfather was a young man with a growing family, he made the decision to move from his home in Positano to America, to work in a bakery. He was going to save money and bring everyone over so they could have a better life. Little did he know that the money he was sending home for their new life in America was being used by his wife to buy up property in Positano! At that time it was a poor fishing village, not the major tourist destination it is today, but she had a vision and set up a hotel called Buca di Bacco. Two generations later, Carla and her siblings Marianna and Sasà now run the century-old family hotel. Carla herself bakes many of the cakes and desserts they serve there. She's one of the best bakers I know. This crostata, or tart, is one of my favorite recipes of hers.

To make the pastry: Sift the flour, baking powder and sugar into a mixing bowl. In a separate bowl, mix the butter, egg yolks, whole egg and lemon zest. Add the wet ingredients to the dry ingredients, and mix to combine. Turn the dough out onto a lightly floured work surface and knead just until it comes together into a smooth dough. Don't overwork it. Roll the dough into a ball, wrap it in plastic and let it rest in the fridge for about an hour.

Preheat your oven to 375°F (190°C). Cut a piece of parchment paper to fit in the bottom of an 9-inch (23 cm) pie plate. Lightly butter the sides of the plate and set aside.

To make the filling: Either by hand or using an electric mixer, whip the egg whites in a bowl with half of the sugar until stiff peaks form. In a separate bowl, mix the remaining sugar, ricotta and lemon zest. Gently fold the egg whites into the ricotta mixture.

Divide the pastry into two portions, one slightly bigger than the other.

Flatten each portion with your hand. Sprinkle a little bit of flour onto your work surface and roll out each disk of pastry. You want to end up with two circles: one large enough to cover the bottom and sides of the pie plate, and a second smaller circle to lay over the top of the filling.

Take the larger circle and press it into the bottom and up the sides of your prepared pie plate. Carefully pour in the filling and level it off so the top is flat. Place the second smaller circle of dough on top and pinch the edges to seal. Cut and discard any excess.

Bake in the oven for about an hour, until golden and firm to the touch.

Remove the pan from the oven and let cool for about half an hour. To unmold, cover the top with a large plate and carefully invert the pie onto the plate. Remove the pan and let the *crostata* cool for another half hour.

Sprinkle the top with icing sugar and serve.

MAKES ONE 9-INCH (23 CM) CROSTATA

LEMON GRANITA

1 cup (250 mL) water

1/3 cup (75 mL) superfine granulated sugar

Rind of 1 lemon, finely chopped

Juice of 3 large lemons

In the heat of the summer, this is about the most refreshing treat you can have. Unlike ice cream, which can be labor-intensive and requires special equipment, granita requires little more than a saucepan, and your freezer does the bulk of the work for you.

In a saucepan over high heat, heat the water and sugar, stirring until the sugar is dissolved. Turn off the heat and let it cool to room temperature. Stir in the lemon rind and lemon juice. Taste it and add more sugar, if necessary.

Pour the mixture into a metal bowl. Freeze for 3 to 4 hours, stirring every 20 minutes or so. The finished granita should be slushy, with bits of frozen lemon rind.

Serve immediately.

MAKES ABOUT 2 CUPS (500 ML)

COOKING WITH MY KIDS

Because I've been talking food and family for so long, I've often been asked for my strategies on feeding kids and handling picky eaters. I've been a little reluctant to say anything—everyone's kids, families and circumstances are unique.

But now as the father of three, and as someone who believes in the link between food, family and tradition, I actually have had some practical hands-on experience at raising kids, and I'm happy to share the bits I've learned.

My wife, Nina, and I were both raised in traditional Italian families, where you were expected to sit at the table and eat what your parents ate. And as our kids transitioned from being toddlers to eating regular food, we tried to carry on that tradition as well. It wasn't always easy, and we had our share of protesting, eye-rolling and sighing, but overall our kids are good eaters who are happy to sit with us at the table.

We've employed some strategies to help teach our kids about food and mealtimes that I can share. Some of these may be obvious, but sometimes it's the most obvious solutions that are the easiest to overlook.

With the amount of travelling I do for work, I constantly worry and feel guilty about whether I'm spending enough really meaningful time with my kids. So when I'm home, we turn dinner preparation time into family time. When Nina and I are making dinner, we get the kids in the kitchen and involve them at whatever level is appropriate, even if it's just setting the table. We're together, having fun and putting our efforts into something we're about to sit down and enjoy together as a family. In my experience, it works. When my kids are involved in making dinner, they're more inclined to eat and they feel proud that they were part of making it. They sit longer at the table and are being subtly taught the value of family time.

Preparing and sharing family meals together serves so many functions beyond just building relationships and memories. Knowing how to cook is about more than just knowing how to feed yourself. The kids are learning to master a life skill, and that helps to build their overall confidence as they go out into the world.

Here are some other strategies: On weekends we take a couple of hours to make some meals or snacks that we can refrigerate or freeze for the week ahead. We often make a double batch of Tomato Sauce (page 19) and either the Ragù Napoletano (page 20) or the Bolognese Sauce (page 23), which can be frozen or refrigerated for use during the week.

Just having the Tomato Sauce at your disposal gives you endless options. You can serve it with a simple pasta, which all kids love. You can make Riso con Salsa di Pomodoro (page 34). You can make soup from it, or simply add some to a soup for extra flavor. You can also make one of our "in a pinch" favorites, Eggs in Purgatory: The kids can pour some of the tomato sauce into a pan, then you heat it up, crack in some eggs, add some slices of cheese like scamorza and cook it, covered, for about 5 minutes, until the eggs have set to your liking.

We also might purée some cooked vegetables and freeze them. This was something Nina came up with when the kids were babies. You cook the vegetables—broccoli, beets, carrots or whatever you'd like—purée in a blender or food processor, then divide the purée into ice-cube trays and freeze. Once they're frozen, you can pop the cubes into freezer bags. Then, midweek, you can quickly add vegetables to any soup or risotto. A risotto with puréed beets is absolute comfort food for my kids.

Rushed midweek meals can become less hurried. And when you pull something out of the fridge that your kids helped to make, they're excited to eat it.

Another great fast dinner cheat is bruschetta. Bruschetta is a thick piece of grilled bread, which is about as simple and economical as it gets. Sometimes on a lazy Sunday night we just heat up our ragù and, instead of pasta, we pour it over big, thick slices of grilled or toasted bread. Or we do bruschetta pizzas, where the kids top their grilled bread with tomato sauce, torn basil and cheese and then melt it in the oven. These are small things, but when you're five, six, seven, it's a big deal. And that empowers them.

In a pinch I go to the local supermarket or pizzeria and buy some pizza dough. Then we get the kids to stretch out the dough and we top our pizzas with our favorite ingredients. Think thin-sliced potatoes, onions and rosemary. Crumbled sausage and gorgonzola. Straight up tomato sauce and oregano. Tomato sauce with tuna, capers, onions. The list goes on and on!

I'd also like to urge you to consider that kids are capable of more than you think. My daughter Emma is really tactile and loves nature. I used to watch her digging in the garden and playing with worms (to Nina's horror!). But based on what I saw, she became my little anchovy helper, cleaning and gutting the fish, when she was about five. Giorgia loves crushing peeled plum tomatoes in a bowl for the tomato sauce, or tasting the pasta to see if it's al dente. The two of them have been working together to make risotto since they were in my arms and I was preparing a meal. They love to stir! Little D (my son, Dante) sees his older sisters engaged and he wants to do it all, too.

In terms of busy nights, I understand the challenges that parents go through. We go through them as well. Making sure your pantry is stocked with the essentials—olive oil, quality tuna, garlic, passata, sundried tomatoes, olives, anchovy fillets and various types of legumes and pasta—means you can have a meal on the table in 15 to 20 minutes. That's way faster than ordering in.

The kids don't know that we're using short cuts and strategies to get meals on the table because we're busy and tired. Or that I'm trying to squeeze in more time with them. What they know is that when we're in the kitchen preparing a meal, that's an open invitation for them to come join in or hang out. Kids naturally want to feel that they have a role to play that is important, and being together in the kitchen gives us the joy of connecting with them, and gives them reassurance that they are contributing.

I started the book talking about how food and family are deep in the Italian psyche and soul. Now that we have kids, our dinner table literally brings our family together.

But the same rules apply to anyone you call family. Invite them over. Bring them into the kitchen while you prepare your meal and then sit together. I guarantee that no matter how humble the food you're serving, the people around it will be like family, even if it's just for the night.

MILLE GRAZIE

To my family: My incredible and beautiful wife, Nina—thank you for steering the ship when I'm away. I couldn't do any of this without you! To my soulmate Emma, my love Giorgia and my prince Dante—I'm so very blessed to have you as my children. You inspire me.

To my brother, Sal, and my sister, Maria: Thanks for being amazing siblings and for being perfectly okay that mom and dad loved me more growing up! My *nonni*, aunts, uncles and cousins, who are way too many to name: Thanks for all the family celebrations with good food, wine and, more often than not, some Rocco craziness.

To all the families I have met over the years, those in this cookbook and the countless others who have shared with me their family recipes and secrets: Your generosity of spirit and your commitment to being the gatekeepers of tradition were incredibly inspiring.

To Kirsten Hanson, my editor: I've probably given you a few sleepless nights with the many curveballs I've thrown your way, but in the end, you made sure I stayed on track. To the team at HarperCollins Canada for being so supportive and for honoring my vision and style. To Tracy Bordian for your meticulous copyediting, and Noelle Zitzer for your precision and patience in making things perfect. And to James Groome for adding a little Dante whenever necessary.

To Joanna McIntyre, creative director at Rockhead Entertainment: Thanks for always being there for me! You're my secret weapon, my advisory board, and you always show me the light. Yes, we are cowboys, and we have tasted the bhang!

To Francesco Lastrucci, my brilliant photographer: When working with you, I'm always reminded that you don't have to be blood-related to be brothers. Your photography is gorgeous and sensual, and captures the heart of what we write about—*Si Gruuooss!* I look forward to our next adventure!

To Katie Blackwell, my trusted second-in-command: You are brilliant! Your design of the book has made this one so special. Thanks for your endless talent and hard work and for making sure everything runs smoothly, even when I'm not around.

Lastly, to Karen Gordon, my "Faux-talian" sister: You know I'm your biggest fan! Thank you for all your hard work in capturing my voice and putting it onto these pages. Your writing has heart and humor, and three books later, you *still* make me laugh.

INDEX